Capital Project Management, Volume I

Capital Project Management, Volume I

Capital Project Strategy

Robert N. McGrath

BEP BUSINESS EXPERT PRESS

Capital Project Management, Volume I: Capital Project Strategy

Cover Image Credit: wichy/shutterstock.com

First published in 2020 by
Business Expert Press, LLC
222 East 46th Street, New York, NY 10017
www.businessexpertpress.com

ISBN-13: 978-1-94999-184-0 (paperback)
ISBN-13: 978-1-94999-185-7 (e-book)

Business Expert Press Portfolio and Project Management Collection

Collection ISSN: 2156-8189 (print)
Collection ISSN: 2156-8200 (electronic)

Cover and interior design by Exeter Premedia Services Private Ltd., Chennai, India

First edition: 2020

10 9 8 7 6 5 4 3 2 1

Printed in the United States of America.

Abstract

The volumes in this series individually and altogether may be likened to a complete case study of Tesla through the end of 2018. *Memorable training and educational learning points are italicized.* Many popular media articles are excerpted, abridged to illustrate points of *theoretical* emphasis. This keeps the story alive, meaningful, and urgent.

Strategic management is a rigorous corpus of scholarship in the Academy of Management, as is technology and innovation management. Project management is found within production or operations management, but is more generally led by the Project Management Institute, a professional trade organization. The volumes in this series intersect conceptually where these fields meet, and in actual practice, where capital projects are planned, budgeted, and financed.

This volume (Volume I) tells the Tesla story and then presents chapters that address, in order: corporate governance and project stakeholder or communication management, project portfolios as strategic corporate portfolios, and an executive-level review of the best-practice project management paradigm, as applied to capital projects. The epilogue takes the story through the end of the first quarter of 2019 and offers commentary with respect to the points made earlier.

Keywords

tesla; musk; pmi; project portfolio; PMO; PMBOK; project communication; project stakeholder; corporate governance; business case; multicriteria assessment; internal corporate venturing; corporate strategy; industry lifecycle; corporate portfolio; capability portfolio; discount rate; hurdle rate; free cash flow

Contents

Preface ix

Chapter 1   Tesla in the Media..1

Chapter 2   Corporate Strategy and Capital Projects.......................15

Chapter 3   Capital Project Portfolios as Strategic
             Corporate Portfolios..39

Chapter 4   Communication and Stakeholder Management............63

Chapter 5   Principles of Project Management................................91

Chapter 6   Epilogue and Conclusion...121

Media Articles 137

References 143

About the Author 147

Index 149

Preface

Strategic Management is a rigorous corpus of scholarship in the Academy of Management, as is Technology and Innovation Management. Project Management is found within Production/Operations Management, but is more generally led by the Project Management Institute, a professional trade organization. The volumes in this series intersect conceptually where all these fields meet, and in actual practice where Capital Projects are Planned, Budgeted, and Financed.

A main premise of this series is that corporations make internal capital investments through a standard budgeting process, where Capital Projects circumscribe the major efforts. For the most part the view in Volume I is Executive. The challenge becomes managing *multiple* Capital Projects, all guided by the same Corporate Strategy. *There, a dynamic Project Management Organization can manage portfolios of projects that are "in synch" with the corporate imperative to create Economic Value-Added in a portfolio of competencies—thus, a PMO as a truly value-adding Organizational Capability.* In the last chapter, the global best-practise approach to managing projects is reviewed, written for executives with the need to understand the Project Management challenge better.

In its totality, this volume takes the view that Project Management has grown from being a set of tools and techniques, and beyond being an *approach* to managing organizations with Capital Projects, to becoming a valid and dominant organizational *function* well-suited to the modern era that demands multi disciplinary innovation as a *core capability* and potential *competitive advantage*.

CHAPTER 1

Tesla in the Media

From Inception into the Early 2000s

In the spring of 2017, the market cap of Tesla reached 59 billion U.S. dollars, compared to 52 billion U.S. dollars for General Motors and 44 billion U.S. dollars for Ford. As the stock price had risen 65 percent in the first few months of 2017 alone, many people thought this was overpriced, but nevertheless, it happened and stunned market-watchers. Reactions to this phenomenon were ambivalent because Tesla was in everyone's mind, at a key point of transition (Tepper 2017). The demand for a mass-market car was still largely hypothetical. Tesla and other players still needed to demonstrate the ability to manufacture electric vehicles (EVs) at large scale. Only by reducing unit costs could the price of an EV come down to what industry wisdom felt was a proper price point (Tepper 2017).

The Tesla story begins around 1990 when Elon Musk was still not in the mix (Baer 2014). A collaboration of Silicon Valley engineers—mainly Malcom Smith and Martin Eberhard—had worked on consumer gadgets and mobility concepts. Soon another joined, a person named Marc Tarpenning. During the late 1990s, they marketed an electronic book, eventually selling the company for 187 million U.S. dollars (Baer 2014). Encouraged, they wanted to start another company, convinced that EVs had a viable future.

They discovered a firm called AC Propulsion that already had a vehicle called the "tzero" (Baer 2014). It was enough for them to invest, but a problem with perceptions was that EVs were something of a joke (McGrath 1996). Technology enthusiasts were interested, as were people concerned about the environment.

Still, it was difficult to envision a profitable market for vehicles, which at the time was quite pricey and underperforming in terms of range.

Range means how far a vehicle can travel on one *fill-up* or here, one re-charging. EVs had poor ranges for a variety of reasons, but none was more important than the energy density of the battery's *type*. Energy density rather readily translates into vehicle range. Also, charging early-generation EVs took hours depending on the voltage at the source, if not overnight. Eventually, though, it all came down to batteries. The founders' enthusiasm was based on advancements in lithium-ion technology (Baer 2014).

2003: Tesla Motors Inc.

The founders incorporated Tesla Motors on July 1, 2003, named, after the famous electrical genius of the 19th century. A prototype EV was ready around 2004. If there was any kind of *breakthrough* about it, it was a novel combination of technologies (Baer 2014). Past that, the team realized that it would have to retrofit an existing car (Baer 2014).

They decided to build on the Lotus Elise, a small sports car. Lotus was a well-established design innovator in racing. Their business terms were attractive to Tesla, and Lotus was used to doing the kind of things that Tesla needed. Tesla was joined by its first Vice President of vehicle development, Ian Wright, the third member of the formal team.

At that point, the main problem became financing, which consumed much of 2004. Tesla needed a major investor who shared their dream. They were familiar with Elon Musk, famous as the founder of SpaceX (Baer 2014). Musk was concerned about the natural environment and believed that EVs could play a role. Musk raised 7.5 million U.S. dollars and became the chairman of the board (COB).

Thus, at the outset, Musk held two important roles, chairman and majority investor.

Tesla's first real product was called the Roadster, released in 2008. It got high praises from sources such as *Car and Driver*. With a bit of trouble about safety and reliability issues, Tesla would enjoy a good public reputation. But making a car from scratch was more difficult than imagined. The partnership with AC Propulsion would, thus, prove fortunate, though in another sense, Tesla passed the chance to learn about building a whole car.

Lotus took the task seriously (Baer 2014). An advantage they held was to not be too integrated with existing suppliers, that is, not to get too *locked-in* to business relationships. They maintained a policy of sourcing along technical superiority. In late 2004, a prototype or *mule* was ready (Baer 2014). The mule was an ungainly Elise, without body panels, but with the hardware and software of an EV. *Proof of concept* was demonstrated. Led by Musk and additional partnering, another 13 million U.S. dollars was raised.

In the spring of 2006, a star-studded event was pulled off in a hangar in Santa Monica CA (Baer 2014). Within a few weeks, Tesla had 127 orders for Roadsters, priced at 100,000 U.S. dollars. Deliveries were scheduled for the summer of 2007. Positive press appeared in the *New York Times, Fortune, Wired,* and the *Washington Post.* However, Elon Musk was not featured well in much of this early publicity, sometimes ignored, and once was misidentified and entirely overlooked. While blaming the press more than his comrades, Musk felt insulted and expressed this in no uncertain terms. *This was not the last time he lashed out at the media.* As the COB, Musk eventually threatened to fire one of the principals. But, regardless of some professional tensions, the team was off to a good start (Baer 2014).

The leaders did not too quickly plan on developing an entire EV. They planned to provide the electronic drive train. Lotus would provide the chassis components and final assembly (Baer 2014). Tesla's portion would be *bolted on* to that. The plan was to begin deliveries of the Roadster in 2006 and continue scaling up production until profitability was reached in 2008. But, it was not ready until 2008, beginning a chronic problem with production (Baer 2014).

The principals were more accustomed to the highly compartmentalized Silicon Valley network's way of doing things.

A story surfaced in the media concerning the top management team (Baer 2014). CEO/Founder Eberhard volunteered to step down to concentrate on technology. The idea received support from the board. *After assuming this role too, his third, Musk started acting somewhat autonomously* (Baer 2014), *taking on tasks more traditional of a chief operations officer, or COO.* Musk made intermittent plant visits, redirecting what people were doing, especially in design (Baer 2014). While the ideas were often good, it was upsetting and helped establish Musk's reputation of being someone who was demanding and difficult to work with.

The search for a replacement CEO began in February 2007, but efforts were unsuccessful (Baer 2014). The media expressed concerns about organizational instability. An important public relations issue was to assure that intramural stresses were nominal, if not normal. A new CEO was named, but from the standpoint of "optics" this was an apparent firing (Baer 2014). Worse, this event was against Tesla's own by-laws, so it was re-accomplished properly and more congenially. The vignette established Musk's reputation for making unconventional moves (Baer 2014). In the summer of 2007, suits and countersuits followed. A permanent CEO was in place in November of 2007, who assured that first Roadster deliveries would begin in the spring of 2008. Sure enough, production began in March of that year. The new CEO lasted until October of 2008, when Elon Musk essentially took over the company, firing about a quarter of Tesla employees.

By that time, Musk himself had invested about 55 million U.S. dollars of his own, which in his mind we might infer, justified being in charge. Tesla was on the verge of collapse by 2008 due to operational cost overruns (Vance 2012). Fortunately, Musk was able to bail out the company in early 2009 with the sale of an earlier venture of his, Everdream, for 120 million U.S. dollars.

By May of 2009, Tesla had recalled 75 percent of the Roadsters sold since March of 2008. Customers were disappointed, which was softened by sending repair technicians to customers' homes to fix the problems. Still, some of the glimmer was off the rose, made worse by several high-profile celebrities announcing their displeasure.

2010: Initial Public Offering

Tesla "went public" in 2010 with a 100 million U.S. dollars initial public offering (IPO), and the public response was enthusiastic. Now "Wall Street" became a major actor. Tesla officials realized that the Roadster was not the future of EVs or the company. They needed a successor, a stepping-stone toward building a mass-market EV—from scratch.

The response was the Model S. As announced in June 2008, the price-point was 60,000 U.S. dollars—still a great deal of money for an under-performing mass-market consumer car. Still, that was only about half of what the Roadster was priced at. A prototype was unveiled in March 2009—the first production cars were not delivered until the middle of 2012 at a price of 106,000 U.S. dollars.

Tesla followers started getting used to this pattern, but now the company was publicly owned. This "public" was not just following the technology, but it was also "following the money." Fortunately, they showed patience.

Truly, it was not surprising that production goals were only partially reached. Experts knew that these timeframes were not unusual. Tesla's estimation by *Wall Street* continued to soar. By the end of 2012, Tesla had only sold a total of about 2,450 cars (Vance 2012). Yet, in late 2014, Tesla's market cap was about 28 billion U.S. dollars (Baer 2014).

Their next car was the Model X, a sports utility vehicle (SUV). True to form, it was promised for first deliveries in 2014, but this did not happen until late 2015. It was priced even higher than the Model S. Originally announced at 80,000 U.S. dollars (Woodyard 2015; Assis March 2016; Rocco 2015), upon first delivery, it was priced at 132,000 U.S. dollars, about 5,000 U.S. dollars more than the Model S.

Tesla buyers showed remarkable loyalty, as the brand capital grew (Sparks 2016). But, brand capital does not always translate into investment capital. EV price was still a large impediment to achieving long-term goals, and that pointed at production costs.

Also, many of the major global auto makers were starting to catch on. Non-U.S. manufacturers would become especially problematic, and their home markets were more sensitive to environmental concerns. The largest market for EVs, by far, would be China.

Tesla's vehicle production facility was in Fremont California (Vance 2012). It was highly robotized, a harbinger of the future of manufacturing. Lithium-ion battery packs were also assembled in the car manufacturing plant. It was unusual for EV manufacturers to be that vertically integrated. Most auto producers outsourced battery production.

Tesla's forward supply chain concept was novel, controversial, and legally challenged in many states (Vance 2012). Rather than having traditional, independent dealerships, Tesla set up a chain of its own *stores*. In a store, a Model S was available for viewing, but not for sale. Stores had interactive touchscreen devices where prospective buyers could fashion a Model S to their own tastes and check pricing. At that time, Tesla was merely taking reservations for a Model S for a refundable down payment of 1,000 U.S. dollars (Vance 2012). The number of reservations became so large as to be a danger sign if Tesla failed to come through.

The obstinate range problem was basically the same that had plagued EVs since the 1800s (Schiffer 1994; Shnayerson 1996; Wakefield 1994). *Range was about as important a consideration as vehicle price. EVs were "just not worth it"—at least not yet.*

Progress also depended on a recharging network, where standardization and public availability were crucial. Tesla set out to build its own network of charging stations. Charging would be free and reasonably fast. This was announced in 2012, but it took some technology development to be fielded (No author "Tesla Unveils," 2012). It was successful enough for Tesla to begin charging a fee in 2017, because by that time, the company could no longer afford to subsidize so many EVs already on the road and growing. Tesla's recharging paradigm was not the only standard, but it was a leading contender.

Signaled by commitments that were global in scope, the prospect of not only creating a dominant design, but also a significant bandwagon effect had implications for Tesla, the EV industry, and socio-economic infrastructures writ large.

On the other hand, it was not certain that lithium-ion batteries would emerge as the *standard* solution for all-battery EVs. For the foreseeable future, most people agreed that hardly anything else was good enough to commercialize a true mass-market EV. Longer term, experts disagreed that any kind of conventional *battery* would become permanent.

Tesla, anyway, was *all in* in lithium-ion batteries and announced the building of *the Gigafactory* in Nevada (Pikkarainen 2016). The facility would be one of the largest factories ever built, and when operating at full capacity, could establish an unassailable unit cost advantage.

Batteries cost about one-third of overall vehicle costs and were needed to be replaced more than once over the life of an EV.

After the Model S was released in 2013, it was awarded the prestigious Motor Trend Car of the Year and quickly outsold other large luxury sedans. This was a remarkable milestone.

Priced at a much improved 50,000 U.S. dollars, the Model S could travel 300 miles on a charge, demonstrating that EVs had made progress in these two foremost metrics (Vance 2012).

In a *tweet* sent on October 1, 2014, Musk announced, in effect, the Model D. The D would have autopilot features. However, naming it *autopilot* was one of the true blunders Tesla made. The word was confused with words like *autonomous* and worsened public perception about a Tesla fatality. Still, in late 2016, *Consumer Reports* would name Tesla the *Most Loved Car Brand* (Sparks 2016), though Tesla's score of 91 percent was below earlier marks in the high marks closer to 100 percent.

The entire global scenario was nearing a critical inflection point. A different kind of auto consumer was entering the market—not quite the mass-market yet, but suggestive of demand to come.

Next came announcements about the Model 3. Tesla was *betting the company*, hoping that it would establish the company as the leader in producing a true mass-market EV that was powered only by batteries (Assis March 2016). Early expectations were for a range of 200 miles, at a list price of 35,000 U.S. dollars. The key questions were, first, would these numbers prove real, and second, prove to be the magic combination of price and performance, together being the real purchase decision criterion? First, deliveries were announced to occur in late 2017.

Looking over its shoulder, Tesla had need to worry about the Chevrolet Bolt also in development. General Motor's (GM's) Bolt was the follow-up on the Chevy Volt, which was a commercial failure, but an invaluable experiment. The Bolt was rumored to have a range of 200 miles on batteries, but that was augmented by a regular engine, and was priced at 37,500 U.S. dollars (Assis March 2016).

2017: Is That Market Cap for *Real?*

Sales of EVs globally were up 30 percent during 2016 (Hoium 2016). Tesla led the way. In the fourth quarter, 22,171 Model S's had been sold (the top seller) as well as 13,448 Model X SUVs (number 3). The Volt was number 2 at about the same point, with 18,517, but the Bolt was the real play to come. Ford's Fusion Energi (also a hybrid) was in fourth place with 13,022 units sold; Nissan sold 10,650 Leafs and in fifth place; and BMW sold 6,205 i3s, in sixth.

Altogether though, sales of hybrids were showing better results than sales of battery-only EVs. Leaders included the Toyota Prius, which could go 56 miles on a gallon of gas and was priced below 25,000 U.S. dollars—dependably, not hypothetically. The Prius stood out amongst 35 other models sold in the United States that surpassed 40 miles per gallon.

Other global companies, especially Volkswagen and Daimler, were announcing massive capital investments. In May, Volkswagen (VW) announced that it would target the sale of one million EVs by 2025. It would directly assault the large volume mass market. VW announced the introduction of 80 EVs by 2025. By 2030, every one of its 300 models (across the VW group) would have electric versions. A single VW platform design named MEB would lead the way. VW's overall financial strategy was to be profitable from the beginning. VW and Tesla would become direct competitors.

Tesla needed to become another kind of company focused on capital-intense, heavy large-scale manufacturing, and managing supply chains of hundreds of suppliers over multiple tiers. Its most intimidating milestone toward accomplishing all of this was to begin—and then sustain—the manufacture of 5,000 Model 3s per week.

In June, Tesla signed a preliminary agreement with the city of Shanghai to look into production in China (No author "Tesla," June 2017). China had already declared EVs to be a national imperative and was developing high-quality suppliers. A downside was that to establish production in China Tesla might have to enter a joint venture agreement. This general issue would continue to get worse. Soon, it had become elevated itself to the national policy level in the United States, a central concern in a trade war. China's position on requiring joint ventures would change in about a year under political pressure.

On July 3 (No author "Tesla Says," July 3, 2017), Tesla said that the Model 3 would go on sale the Friday of the same week. The price point was 35,000 U.S. dollars after a 7,500 U.S. dollars tax credit and would have a rage of 215 miles.

But, on the same day (No author "Chevrolet," July 3, 2017), GM announced that its sales of Bolts in June was the highest monthly total so far, 1,642 cars and up 5 percent in one month. Its price was 37,500 U.S. dollars and had a rage of 238 miles, granting GM some bragging rights as well as augmenting its reputation in mass markets. Head-to-head competition between the Model 3 and the Bolt now seemed unmistakable, even if it was not openly admitted. At least, Tesla needed to ramp-up production to keep pace with Bolt sales, and GM still had not rolled out the Bolt nationally. GM planned to double the production of Bolts to 30,000 a year, with some time and difficulty (No author "Chevrolet," July 3, 2017).

Later, the same year, Daimler announced plans to electrify its whole fleet by 2020, investing 11 billion U.S. dollars in the effort (Muoio 2017). They would form a joint venture with the Chinese auto manufacturer SAIC, a major upcomer and government darling. Tesla was already popular among the Chinese well-to-do, but Daimler and others felt that they were better positioned to enter *late* so to speak. Clearly, China was the major battleground.

Major announcements kept coming. Honda announced a platform that would underpin a line of EVs targeted at Europe; by 2030, it intended to have two-thirds of sales revenues generated by electrics (No author "Honda," September 14, 2017). Jaguar said that, by 2020, all its models would be either all-electric or hybrid (Gastelo 2017). BMW's challenge would be the i5 sedan. Toyota announced that by the early 2020s, it would field 10 electrified vehicles, and that by 2025, there would be an electric version of every model in its line (Kageyama 2017).

To accomplish this, Toyota would source batteries through a partnership with Panasonic. Panasonic was also the supplier of batteries to Tesla. In September, VW supported a consortium of European battery manufacturers. At the time, VW sourced its batteries from LG Chem and Samsung of Korea (No author "VW," September 2017). Globally, many advanced battery developments continued to be researched. As usual, scaling up to economical mass-production volumes was a big challenge. In short, the structure of the battery industry was evolving a different shape than the top tier of auto manufacturers.

The writing was also on the wall about vehicle automation combined with electrification. There, institutional markets were being targeted as testing grounds for eventual mass markets, but mainstream consumers were clearly foreseeable.

By the U.S. holiday season, summations about Tesla usually read like this:

(DeBord November 25, 2017).

From a return-on-investment-capital standpoint, Tesla is a catastrophe, while GM is a triumph. GM has been making money for years and is now seeing its stock climb ... Tesla just notched the biggest quarterly loss in the company's 14-year history.

That said, Tesla continues to enjoy a $50-billion-ish market cap (larger than Ford and Fiat Chrysler Automobiles) and a seemingly endless appetite for new capital raises and more recently, debt issuance ... Investors don't care about this stuff, however. That's because the Tesla story is just too enticing.

2018: *Production Hell*

By going from niche markets to the mass market, Tesla had awakened the global auto incumbency. All players were collectively creating a mutually ruinous condition of production overcapacity—not only batteries and Gigafactories, but vehicles themselves.

Tesla was also drawing closer to no longer being eligible for the 7,500 U.S. dollars tax credit that U.S. buyers of EVs could take (Edgerton 2018). Each automaker was allowed to sell 200,000 EVs before its limit was exhausted, but Tesla would meet that total by the middle of the year. As Tesla approached its limit, newer entrants still had plenty of room before reaching 200,000.

Dominating news about Tesla, though, was its ability to produce Model 3s and meet the goal of producing 5,000 per week. Production was then about 2,500 per week. This capacity was as important to satisfying customers with reservations, as it was to investors. Tesla was *burning capital* at one billion U.S. dollars per quarter.

Musk then startled onlookers by saying that the company had gone bankrupt—as an April Fool's joke. This was not funny on *Wall Street.* Within days, Musk promised that Tesla would not borrow more capital that year and would begin positive cash flow in the third quarter. *The Economist,* however, said that Tesla would need as much as three billion U.S. dollars (Barrabi 2018). Tesla's bonds were downgraded to junk.

Tesla's access to capital was one thing, but another issue was the cost of (the) capital raised, which was going up. It is a serious threat to making positive capital project returns and, in turn, overall corporate earnings.

As April turned into May, the corporate world was stunned as Tesla shareholders voted on a proposal to oust Musk as chairman (Barrabi 2018). At the June meeting, the ouster coup was rebuffed. However, the affair was a wake-up call. The *media narrative* changed, and Musk's relationship with it began to disintegrate: "Tesla was making it difficult for even 'believers' to own the company's stock. Musk responded that investors worried about volatility should steer clear of Tesla's shares" (No author "Tesla," 2018). Musk was becoming even more embittered by Tesla stock short-sellers. The amount of Tesla stock *sold short* was reaching record levels, as did the level of Musk's public testiness about it.

Musk began overseeing production at the Freemont plant. Progress was made in fits and starts, at times alternating between planned stoppages, unplanned stoppages, and maximum effort (Sage 2018). In a lengthy interview, Musk mused about the past as well as going forward:

(Randall July 13, 2018).

You don't really know that you can actually handle a given rate unless you try to do it. So we successively hit limitations in general assembly, in paint, in body, in module production, pack production, logistics …

… There are parts of it that are completely automated … And then there are parts of it which are completely manual … Then there are parts that are partly automated and partly manual.

… You can only move as fast as the slowest thing in the system … Part of the problem is that the designing heads were naive about manufacturing.

Patience with Tesla was wearing thin in some stakeholder camps.

Goldman Sachs said that Tesla would need to raise another 10 billion U.S. dollars in the upcoming two years just to survive. "Musk simply said 'No … I specifically don't want to'" (Franck 2018). Any words at all from a person like Musk could move markets. The daily heartbeat on *Wall Street* is largely driven by such statements, as well as whether its expectations are met.

As June turned into July and despite all distractions, Tesla did indeed, but with much unusual effort, manage to produce 5,000 Model 3s in a week. Still, observers were relentless:

(Krishner July 2, 2018).

… The Model 3, which starts at $35,000, is the key to turning Tesla from a niche maker of expensive electric cars to a profitable, mass-market automaker. The company badly needs cash …to post a net profit and positive cash flow in the third and fourth quarters. The company has had only two profitable quarters in its 15-year history …

Moody's … downgraded Tesla's debt into junk territory back in March, warning that Tesla won't have cash to cover $3.7 billion for normal operations, capital expenses and debt that comes due early next year. Tesla said cash from Model 3 sales will pay the bills and drive profits.

On Twitter, Musk next announced that Tesla had secured the funding needed to take the corporation back to private ownership. This way, existing stockholders would be rewarded for their patience, their shares bought back at a premium, and then they would be bid farewell forever. Doing so would liberate Musk to run his company. However, rumors immediately broke that this was done as much to frustrate the short-sellers, because the Tweet alone caused an immediate jump in the stock price. Funding was promised, so it was said from a Saudi source that proved to lack the credibility needed to keep the U.S. Securities and Exchange Commission (SEC) from investigating. The issue was quickly settled by Musk agreeing to pay a hefty fine and to be replaced as CEO. This was not the last of his public feud with the SEC.

For the third quarter of 2018, Tesla announced its third-ever quarterly profit. However, it would take more than that one quarter's results and made on a more consistent basis, before stakeholders would become convinced this was evidence of long-term economic profitability. Tesla had also become symbolic for hopes about the profitability of EVs in general, which would be received with ambivalence. After all, some stakeholder groups were still hoping that Tesla would fail and just go away.

That was the good news! The bad news was that Tesla became accused of criminally overstating production forecasts for the Model 3, or in other words, misleading the expectations of stakeholders before and during the recent profitable quarter. That fueled cynics about Tesla's profits and longer-term expectations, who could assert that the recent earnings report was perhaps not technically phony, but something of an accounting canard.

(Heisler November 16, 2018).

... one of the reasons why Tesla's ability to ramp up Model 3 production has drawn so much scrutiny over the past few months is because Musk has a bad habit of making ambitious promises regarding production that often go unfulfilled ... While the company can pull out all the stops and have an incredibly high production rate in any given week, history has shown that keeping such production levels consistent across many weeks is far more challenging.

From another point of view, signs of hope were that: 61,394 Model 3s were produced in the fourth quarter, and about 1,000 per day were delivered. This calculates to 5,000 per week, though there were anecdotal reports to the contrary. Still, in the year, 254,240 Teslas of all kinds were delivered, including 145,846 Model 3s and 99,394 of the Models Ss and Xs (No author "Tesla,"1919). But, always lurking:

(Assis January 2, 2019).
By
Claudia
Reporter
Tesla Inc. ... is still basking in the afterglow of the profit reported for its latest quarter.

...The analysts ... envision a virtuous cycle: as Tesla delivers steady cash flow, "a new group of investors will begin taking positions, helping drive shares higher ..."

"The lead is theirs to squander," said [an official] ... And there's "no limit to demand, (Tesla) can sell them as much as it can make them," because ... Teslas are a delight to drive.

A few weeks later, Tesla announced that it would reduce the full-time workforce by 7 percent. The company realized it needed to move from expensive versions of the Model 3 to less-expensive models, aiming at a price point (before subsidies) of 35,000 U.S. dollars.

That price point would finally be achieved in the early months of 2019, but not without a healthy dose of skepticism, given Tesla's track record.

The last chapter in this book provides an epilogue and concludes—for the time being.

CHAPTER 2

Corporate Strategy and Capital Projects

Introduction

Strategic management is a rigorous corpus of research and scholarship in business administration. If one is to speak of capital projects, one should have a grasp of strategic management imperatives. This is because by definition, capital projects deploy investor capital. The connection between externally borrowed capital and any specific project budget may not be plain, but it exists nonetheless and is only a matter of accounting logic to deduce. This chapter elaborates on that theme by *connecting the dots* between the *C Suite* and the capital project manager. The focus is on the correct use of meaningful terms, not as a matter of semantics, but for precise conveyance of key ideas that resonate throughout this book and others in this series.

After Studying this Chapter, the Reader will be Able to:

Define and give an example of a corporate portfolio of competencies and organization wide capabilities.

Define *competitive advantage* and explain why economic value added correctly measures the ultimate success of a business strategy (as opposed to a corporate strategy).

Explain the distinction between traditional financial portfolio diversification and modern corporate portfolio diversification as they pertain to strategic goals.

Explain return on investment and draw the distinction between an operational expense and a capital investment.

Define cash flow and explain free cash flow.

Corporate Portfolio Candidates

For illustration and context, this section blends a fuller elaboration of the Tesla story with enough explanation to carry the conversation forward.

In the vocabulary of strategic management, the word *corporate* connotes both a level of management and an approach to developing a portfolio of businesses. Historically, a corporate portfolio was viewed largely in financial terms, in much the same way that a personal investment portfolio is viewed. There, diversification optimizes the pros and cons of risk and return. *In the modern era, however, that view has moved aside to the view that a corporate portfolio be centered on a common set of competencies and capabilities. Past that, technologies are, first and foremost, human competencies and organization wide capabilities.* This idea is consistent in both the engineering and management disciplines (Betz 2003).

With that background, and given the finite amount of affordable capital that Tesla had and might be able to obtain, a question emerges: What combination of the following (even without considering anything else) would comprise a portfolio of capital projects that together would return more to stockholders than, theoretically, any other combination?

Batteries

One way to assess technological progress on a macro level is to monitor patents. This happened in the Tesla story, though the emphasis on patents was often subtle:

(Lienart and White January 18, 2018).

... GM was issued 661 U.S. patents on battery technology from 2010 through 2015 ... trailing only Toyota's 762 battery patents among global automakers.

... GM's strategy to reduce battery cost is not tied to a single improvement such as a change in battery chemistry, but rather a series of continuous enhancements in battery technology and packaging ...

"There's a lot of stuff that we choose not to patent because we don't want to make it visible" before the new technology goes into production.

The above reflected a big *capital investment* in battery production, but one that was not entirely predictable. The broader picture is partly filled in by articles like this:

(Alton February 21, 2018).

… when lithium-ion batteries emerged on the market, they quickly became the dominant model. The energy density of lithium-ion batteries more than double the standard nickel-cadmium equivalent, with potential for even higher energy densities …

… organizations will continue focusing on iterative improvements to the standard lithium-ion battery model. Until enough investors start to stake riskier projects and invest in potentially game-changing breakthroughs, we'll remain in this temporary valley of advancement.

The so-called *battery* of individual electrochemical cells had not changed much since its original invention well over a century earlier. Everything done to them since was incremental compared to technologies such as fuel cells, photovoltaics, and ultracapacitors. An example was the shift in the early 1990s from nickel-cadmium (NiCad) to lithium. Even at that time, the *energy density* (roughly speaking, the amount of *juice* that translates directly into electric vehicle (EV) range) of lithium technology was twice that of NiCad, with clear room for improvement. The basic construction was also simpler and could be stored for longer periods. But, lithium technology was relatively fragile, for example, the circuitry needed protection. Then, there was the fire hazard that simply did not exist with other technologies. Advancements in one battery parameter (energy density, recharging time, recharging cycle limits, size, weight, and of course, cost) can injure progress (or even cause regression) in another parameter.

Trade-offs in functional performance parameters *is common in technology development (e.g., R&D) writ large.*

There simply was no perfect battery, or at least there was no perfect one-size-fits-all solution. They each needed to be designed with specific operating environments and the demands of particular applications in mind. As such, there were always reports and rumors of better batteries being developed in the lab stage, touting their natural potentials, but almost always, with the disappointing caveat that they faced scale-up and other commercialization problems that about as often, were unique to specific applications and markets.

Industrial history shows that this kind of problem—a predicate to profitable manufacture-ability, crudely called "scaling up"—is almost inevitable.

The *big technological breakthrough* was always in the future, and indeed, always seemed to be right around the corner—so much the case that one was forced to doubt that there was any such thing as a *breakthrough* at all. For example,

(Mims March 18, 2018).

... The next wave of batteries, long in the pipeline, is ready for commercialization ... As this technology becomes widespread, makers of electric vehicles and home storage batteries will be able to knock thousands of dollars off their prices over the next five to 10 years ...

... [But] There is a limit to how far lithium-ion batteries can take us; surprisingly, it's about twice their current capacity. The small, single-digit percentage improvements we see year after year typically are due to improvements in how they are made ... What's coming is a more fundamental change to the materials that make up a battery ...

Well, let us hope so, because stories like that seemed *apropos* to many preceding decades, almost word-for-word. For the time being, anyway, that article went on to detail the replacement of graphite with silicon as the basic material in lithium battery anodes, with many times more *room* for ions. True to form, there were caveats: "The trick is, silicon brings with it countless technical challenges. For instance, a pure silicon anode will soak up so many lithium ions that it gets 'pulverized' after a single charge" (Mims 2018). The nanotechnology was proprietary, but several new, young firms were pursuing it, with predictions of up to 40 percent more energy storage. Factoring in things like a space trade-off, EVs might see a 30 percent range increase.

The strategist should then muse, "at what point, if ever, should I abandon my existing technology that seems exhausted, and commit to one like this with greater natural potential?"

One level of analysis up, equally interesting were advancements in solid-state battery technology, where the traditional liquid electrolyte was replaced by a solid (i.e., a different meaning than many people will recall from earlier days of vacuum tubes and consumer electronics, *transistor radios* etc.). Continuing:

(Eisenstein January 1, 2018).

... Solid state technology is expected to make big leaps ... packing in at least twice the power in a given size of battery ... [the] energy density ... that could more than double again.

That would let an automaker halve the size of its battery pack for the same range – or deliver at least double the distance between charges. Or they could strike a balance ...

The new technology ... replaces the liquid electrolyte ... with ceramic materials. That's yet another plus because the liquid in lithium-ion cells is as flammable as gasoline.

That sounds too good to be true, which is correct for strategic purposes because a capital commitment would need time and deep pockets. *"[T]the technology works in the lab. Now they must ensure they can mass produce the batteries and then show they can survive ... the new formulation probably won't be in widespread use until the middle of the coming decade"* (Eisenstein 2018). Thus, some major players were named, along with a few relative startups in various forms of collaboration: BMW, Toyota, Mazda, and Panasonic (already making Tesla batteries). Altogether, then, if a firm wanted to make EVs, waiting around for the perfect battery was likely a fool's errand. By early 2018, the market share in the early mass-market phase was already taking shape with the Bolt and the Model 3, both based on lithium-ion though Musk, of course, always bragged that Tesla's technology was leading-edge.

"First-mover advantage" is not guaranteed by fast time-to-market, and "fast-followers" often prove wisest in the long run.

But, in the present case, strategies that postponed entry very much longer would likely miss the change to participate in the development of *network externalities* and a *dominant design* (later chapter). The story was one for the ages and still anything but fait accompli for Tesla or anyone else. At any rate and probably for the reminder of the decade, any commercializeable battery EV (BEV) needed to be designed around lithium. Highly conveniently for Tesla and most others, at about that time, a logistical situation concerning lithium constraints reversed itself. The world had plenty of lithium it now seemed, though extraction technologies varied (somewhat analogous to the way crude oil might be extracted from shale, sand, undersea, etc.), and the global infrastructure would need much expansion for EVs alone.

It is difficult to overstate the implications of this relief for battery suppliers and EV designers alike, and the EV movement on the whole. As it concerned Tesla, related was its commitment to lithium battery technology not only in its vehicle designs, but again, in massive, *capital-intense* but *asset-specific* (later chapter) facility commitments like the enormous Gigafactory. Moreover, back a bit into 2017, consider:

(Shane November 20, 2017).

"Whoever controls the lithium supply chain will control the future of the electric vehicle space … There's a global battery arms race" …

… China produces about two-thirds of the global supply of batteries for electric vehicles … building about half of the 20 or more battery mega-factories currently in the works …

And it's not just lithium that China's locking down.

Cobalt, another metal used to make electric vehicle batteries, is even scarcer.

Cobalt was an even more costly ingredient for some EV batteries. Shortages were predicted to occur by 2020, which was not far away in terms of the needed exploration, extraction, and supply chain development:

(Nelson December 18, 2017).

[Cobalt,] ... mined as a by-product of copper and nickel, is a crucial element in the lithium-ion batteries that power everything from electric cars to Apple products ...

The metal's popularity is inherently problematic ... two-thirds of the world's cobalt is in the Democratic Republic of Congo. Political instability and reports of child labor ... have seen some mining companies leave the country.

Other nations were being courted for exploration and sourcing by as many as 100 companies globally, up from only 30 in 2015 (Rodriguez 2018). First, though, an ironic condition of oversupply would likely happen for a few years before shortages became serious. The commodity price for cobalt thus was becoming volatile, because commodity prices are highly sensitive to such news. In conditions like this, volume buyers (like Tesla and its suppliers) often embark on *hedging* procurement strategies; for example, locking in good prices in return for guaranteed large-volume purchases. This is proper financial management, but it stresses the importance of any EV *design* commitments.

In short, and working backwards through the logic:

If mass markets are the target, low unit costs are imperative;

Since mass markets are large by definition, that goes hand-in-hand with mass production;

The two, together, point to the necessity of finding and exploiting (not the same) economies of scale;

Economies of scale usually incur large capital investments in either large facilities or high-tech production equipment, and often both;

Such large commitments are risky to the extent that there is "asset specificity" in the property, plant, and equipment involved;

These risks can be reduced once technology standards have been (practically) established and dominant designs (formal/institutional or de facto*) look to be dependable (at least for the duration of the capital investment horizon);*

Timing (of Technological Discontinuities,) not just time-to-market (of specific products), is critical when making commitments to technology (product and production);

First-Mover Advantage (the preclusion of effective competitive reactions) and Cost of Capital is at stake, as are the Competitive Advantage(s) they imply (especially in combination).

These statements focus on obtaining and sustaining a competitive advantage as the result of a business strategy, a strategy circumscribed by the boundaries of a single industry, which will be explained next.

As these discussions continue, the implications of these strategic realities for capital project management will be explicated.

Stored Power

The word *battery* implies human competencies in the science of electrochemistry and broad organizational capabilities in products that include both EV batteries and things like Tesla's Powerwall. The SolarCity acquisition by Tesla had a nepotistic character, but that did not make it unwise. More arguable was whether the marriage of the science of photovoltaics and solar panels was synergistic with the science of electrochemistry and batteries. It would make sense if viewed from the *product* end, because solar tiles were limited unless the solar energy could be stored in another product like the Powerwall.

The point is to draw the distinction between a product market and an organization as a set of competencies and capabilities.

Modern strategic thinking begins with an emphasis on what can be directly, internally managed, but from there welcomes external opportunities with open arms. To illustrate, it does well to overall media accounts during 2017 and 2018. To start:

(Kharpal May 10, 2017).

Tesla has been branching out beyond just its electric cars to other sustainable energy products. It acquired SolarCity last year, another company founded by Musk, which focused on solar power and energy storage. Tesla makes a product called Powerwall as well as commercial solar panels.

"The goal is to have ... solar roofs that look better than normal roof, generate electricity, last longer, have better insulation and actually have a cost, an installed cost that is less than a normal roof plus the cost of electricity."

That same day:

(Bomey May 10, 2017).

... "pilot manufacturing" would begin at its Fremont, Calif., [EV] factory in the second quarter.

The product, which Tesla will offer through its SolarCity division, will be a no-brainer for homeowners, Musk has said ...

"Solar and batteries go together like peanut butter and jelly," Musk said in October.

Perhaps, and that had an additional relevance:

(Paul September 28, 2017).

... construction has started on building the world's biggest battery to help keep the lights on in Australia's most wind-dependent state.

Tesla ... won a bid in July to build a 129 megawatt hour (MWh) battery and the state is counting on it to be ready ... when electricity demand begins to peak ...

... the battery ... should cost around $750 to $950 per kilowatt, or up to $95 million ... the cost to Tesla would be "$50 million or more" if it failed to deliver the project on time ...

Before long:

(Williams November 22, 2017).

Tesla power packs have now been fully installed on a site near a wind farm north of Adelaide and will be tested to ensure the battery meets standards laid down by the energy market operator ...

Musk is building the world's largest lithium-ion battery system to help the state avert crippling electricity blackouts ... The futurist chief executive made a bet on Twitter in March that he could install a 100-megawatt storage facility within 100 days or it would be free, and the clock started ticking ... when the contract was signed.

Musk's promise was kept on time, leaving Tesla in a good position in one of the world's largest and most promising markets for products *within its capabilities*. In the context of managing innovation, those three words—markets, products, and capabilities—go together like peanut butter and jelly—and do not forget the bread.

Managing technological innovation well means managing a three-part challenge of managing markets, technologies-competencies, *and* organizational capabilities.

However, in other ways, the SolarCity business seemed lacking and in need of attention if its global reputation for customer service was deemed important. The problem was not unlike that also developed in EV *stores*, but seemed more severe:

(Matousek June 26, 2018).

... Between its electric vehicles, home charging units, solar panels, and home batteries, [Tesla] offers customers the opportunity to buy into an integrated system of products ...

But for ... its Powerwall home battery and solar roof ... the company has left its customers and salespeople wondering when the products will arrive ...

...The Powerwall is an important point of differentiation for Tesla, as most of its competitors in the solar panel production business don't make home batteries ...

Tesla's solar roof ... is a major selling point for the company. It was designed to be more aesthetically pleasing than typical solar panels and more durable.

The lesson is that marketers will hasten to remind technology and production people that the forward supply chain, ending in customer service, is every bit as important as the backward supply chain, starting with mineral extraction. Here was a *capability* where Tesla was evidently lacking— *end-to-end supply chain management*, despite Musk's boasts of vertical integration at the factory. But, the broader point applies this thinking to the overall corporate portfolio, not of product lines and industries served, but something intrinsic to the organization itself. Identifying and managing an overall capability requires a person to think organization wide.

A capability might consist of any combination of intangible resources, tangible resources, and human competences, and think of one as being a complex organizational amalgam, a production (sub)system that adds value.

Think of an exemplary corporation as one that has

(a) *a strategy,*
(b) *technologies-competencies and an overall capability,*
(c) *that is/are the cause of high profitability, which hence and only hence,*
(d) *is the corporate-wide basis for superior financial performance and returns to owners.*

These statements largely pertain to corporate *strategy based on broad-based capabilities that cross lines of business, more so than a single-business strategy focused on competitive advantage.*

Later, this will serve as backdrop for justifying an investment in a project management organization.

The Tesla Semi

In a story that was first announced during 2017, its importance seemed to grow into 2018:

(Sparks April 28, 2017).

… Up until now, all that was known about Tesla Semi is that it would be unveiled in September, and that … the semi would "deliver a substantial reduction in the cost of cargo transport" …

... Tesla ... is now including sensors in all of its vehicles that will eventually enable them to drive autonomously Opens a New Window.—even without a driver in the vehicle.

... the market for semis is large enough to represent a revenue opportunity in excess of $100 billion annually for Tesla.

A few months later:

(Vartabedian August 24, 2017).

... That audacious effort could open a potentially lucrative new market ...

Or it could prove an expensive distraction. Musk in July warned that the company is bracing for "manufacturing hell" as it accelerates production of its new Model 3 sedan.

In November, observers were wowed at an event where not only the semi was unveiled, but out of its trailer sprung, a new Roadster with a 600-mile range, by far the longest of any available all-battery EV:

(Sage November 17, 2017a).

... Some analysts fear the truck will be an expensive distraction for Tesla, which is burning cash, has never posted an annual profit, and is in self-described "manufacturing hell" starting up production of the $35,000 Model 3 sedan ...

Tesla would need to invest substantially to create a factory for those trucks. The company is currently spending about $1 billion per quarter, largely to set up the Model 3 factory, and is contemplating a factory in China to build cars.

As the story continued into 2018, it became apparent that Tesla's opportunities would not go uncontested. But before reading the following excerpt, recall that while fuel cells had always suffered size limitations, they had already been fielded in larger vehicles such as urban buses. Then again, urban buses do not voyage far from their motor pools and refueling points:

(Rocco January 30, 2018a).

Nikola Motor Company ... plans to build a $1 billion plant in Arizona ...

The plant will become one of the largest manufacturing facilities dedicated to next-generation semi-trucks ... Navistar and Volkswagen are also working on electric medium-duty trucks.

Nikola ... is developing two electric semi-trucks powered by hydrogen fuel cells and has received pre-orders for more than 8,000 big rigs.

In a few months:

(Rocco May 03, 2018b).

... Anheuser-Busch ... has placed an order for up to 800 hydrogen-powered semi trucks made by Nikola Motor, which is competing against Tesla ...

The Nikola trucks will be able to travel from 500 to 1,200 miles on one hydrogen fuel tank ... The tanks can be refilled in 20 minutes.

... The company has now booked nearly $9 billion in pre-orders.

And, from the global incumbency:

(Rosevar June 28, 2018).

Daimler ... said that two big-truck operators, Penske Truck Leasing and NFI Industries, have agreed to begin using two all-new electric Freightliner trucks in a pilot program ...

... Tesla doesn't appear to have made any effort to finish [its] Semi's development ...

And given its all-out effort to get production of its compact sedan up to speed, it seems unlikely that Tesla's engineers have had much bandwidth to work on the Semi.

Time and again, and on behalf mostly of investment communities, the media refocused attention on the Model 3 as the urgency of most pressing business concern.

Should Tesla diminish as a viable business investment, its leadership of all stakeholder groups would fade proportionately and, perhaps, fatally.

That is not all that Elon Musk and Tesla had in mind. For one thing, they do not even consider subsequent vehicle models (like a pickup truck) and updates to existing ones (e.g., autonomous technology). And of course, there was *productizing the factory* with advances in robotics, artificial intelligence, and the rest. After all, these matters were really at the heart of what Tesla had always envisaged itself as a corporation—affordable all-battery EVs for the everyday mass market consumer. Or were they?

The key words are "envisaged itself as a corporation."

The next section articulates the modern view of that idea and serves as a transition between strategic management of corporate portfolios at the executive level and managing coordinated portfolios of capital projects in a dedicated way.

The Strategic Meaning of a Diversified Portfolio

One of the worst and unfortunately, commonest abuses of business jargon is the term "competitive advantage."

The correct application matters to portfolio management at all levels, as a matter of applying the correct goal-sets and metrics of success. The main area of confusion concerns the distinction between *corporate strategy* and *business strategy*.

Business Strategy and Competitive Advantage

Profitability correctly refers to the inherent or economically structural ability to turn a profit, on average, across a population of firms normally called the industry.

This *economic ability* is regardless of whether any one company decides to declare a profit at any time or say, reinvest positive margins into expansion projects, research and development (R&D), and the like. Tesla would decide on taking the reinvestment route, despite reaching a likely structural level of positive profitability, had the strategy been more short-term, contained, and modest in its goals. Investors would keenly notice, but despite continued losses, maintained faith in the long run.

In the present case, the correct course depended on understanding the typical characteristics of *pioneer market niches*, as opposed to mainstream or *mass-market segments* (Baer 2014). Pioneer markets are more tolerant about *bugs* in early models of truly innovative products, sometimes willing to be unofficial *beta* testers as a matter of fun! Pioneer markets are also less price-sensitive, whereas mainstream segments have a better feel for should-cost pricing. Mainstream segments, by definition, have little of such patience, and in fact, sophisticated mainstream segments can favor ancillary parameters like reliability, maintainability, and even resale value.

Competitive advantage is not a matter of opinion! (Besanko, Dranove and Stanley 2003; Porter 1980). *Its definition and measure are matters of economic rigor.*

Long-term, sustained economic value-added (EVA) is prima facia evidence that a firm has a competitive advantage in its industry and only in its industry.

EVA or economic profit, is basically accounting profit (earnings) less costs of capital that do not appear on income statements and balance sheets.

From there, the analysis turns to where inside the firm the advantage really lies. The prevailing view is that the locus of competitive advantage lies is a firm's competences and capabilities (Hamel and Prahalad 1994). A competence is low-level and confined or local, while a capability is organization wide and more holistic, and generally multi disciplinary.

Long-term profitability at the firm level depends on establishing and sustaining a competitive advantage grounded in an organization wide capability.

Corporate Strategy and Shareholder Wealth

When an organization competes in more than one business, market, or industry, its topmost plan is said to be the corporate strategy, regardless of what its organization chart looks like or what legal form it has chosen, that is, an organization does not have to be a legal corporation, an *Inc.*, to compete across business lines. For a while, Tesla still was a *car company* even after it had already *gone public*—at least in the minds of many.

At the multidivisional corporate level, the strategic issue shifts from profitability and competitive advantage in only one industry, to maximizing returns to shareholders by operating in several industries (Adjaoud, Charfi and Chourou 2011; Baker and English 2011; Ferreria 2011).

The practical issue is whether a corporation can get better financial results by managing several lines of business under the corporate umbrella, or not.

The management challenge is to develop a corporate portfolio of businesses such that altogether, they achieve superior results as a portfolio—a "sum of the parts" versus synergy problem.

On the other hand, the days when corporations were viewed purely as financial portfolios are largely gone. The general public is about as well-informed as corporate managers and about as capable of efficiently allocating their own capital as corporate managers can on their behalf. This does not say that the information is perfectly *symmetric* though. Certainly, internal managers know a lot more than the general public knows. The point is that, as far as it concerns making rational and timely investment decisions, and because so much corporate information must be made public anyway, external investors know quite enough to make good decisions about a publicly traded firm. Moreover, *retail* investors can do this at almost no cost, *especially when compared to the costs of running corporate management infrastructures.* Corporate executives now need a different argument, one that is more comprehensively strategic than exclusively financial.

Corporate portfolios should make sense not by dint of extensive diversification such as one might find in a mutual fund, IRA or 401(k), but by a commonality across business divisions in their competencies and capabilities that may not even be apparent on the surface. Just identifying these takes active and technologically savvy management, which is where managers should be able to outperform external investors. In this way, a corporate echelon of management may justify its costly existence, even when compared to public investment infrastructures that get more efficient all the time (Hart 1993; Rosen 1993).

Metrics Where Corporate Meets Project Management

Often, commonly used terms of importance are misapplied simply because they have different meanings at two levels of management—now, corporate management and project management. *Portfolio* is one, and this is no mere matter of theoretical semantics. A corporate portfolio is not *necessarily* a project portfolio (explained as follows,) but in the abstract, there is scant reason to dismiss the possibility. To argue this carefully, right now, it is best to draw key distinctions among a few measures of success. The purpose of this section is merely to expose the potential for confusion among practicing managers; Volume II of this series provides much more extensive discussions.

Return on Investment

Just saying returns or returns on an investment is not the same thing as using the abbreviation ROI, which denotes a specific formula (which differs anyway from one application to the next). In any case, however, the general idea would be to measure of *return* over-and-above the full return of an amount of principle invested, divided by that amount invested.

ROI (uppercase or lowercase) is only positive after the principle, the amount invested, is fully returned, and is measured as a percentage or a ratio, not a sum.

Stated differently, any positive cash inflow (e.g., sales revenue) that falls short of fully remunerating the investment (a cash outflow) results in a *negative* ROI. A common error is to blithely think of just about any worthwhile expense as an investment and to think of any positive cash inflow as the return.

This is a very bad error because it confuses an expense and an investment, and the nature of projects differs identically from the very top level of capital budgeting.

Cost of Capital and Capital Risk

Again, capital projects are funded through the capital budget, which together with ordinary-expensed projects found in the operating budget, comprise the top-level master budget. Capital projects are investments that rightfully expect positive returns.

Borrowing from investors, whether in the form of equity or stock, debt or bonds, or anything else, does not happen without compensation for several kinds of risk.

Most simple, perhaps, is liquidity risk, or the loss to the investors of the immediate *control* of their principle. Another is principle risk, or the simple risk that investors will not get their *money back*, that being the actual dollar sum that they invested regardless of any additional returns to it. Then, of course, is the return risk, or the risk they will not get the return on their investment that they expect.

Sometimes, the return is determined legal covenant, as in the case of the guaranteed interest on corporate bonds. (This is the *nominal* rate for bonds, the rate that is printed on the bond.) Sometimes, it is more general and carries no guarantee, so terms other than *interest* are needed, such as dividends on common stock and capital appreciation (rising stock prices) over time. Capital appreciation is a return too, but it does not really cost the corporation anything in the immediate sense, aside *expectations* and what they compel a firm to do.

Of the ways any firm might obtain financing, the most popular ways are: borrowing from banks, expansion of short-term liabilities, selling marketable securities, selling assets or even whole parts of the business, issuing additional bonds, preferred stock, or common stock, or of course, using the positive margins generated by current operations (Bierman and Schmidt 2006). Funds generated by operations mostly refer to positive operating margins or gross margins, that is, positive cash flows prior to be being adjusted downward on income statements for things like income taxes and then, finally reported as accounting profit.

After that, that is, when adjusted downward again for the costs of capital, the result is EVA, which is not obliged to be reported.

Opportunity Cost (of Capital)

Other than declare dividends to be taken from the accounting profit, a firm may choose to keep some or all of it so that the funds can be used in the future, to make future capital investments. If funds are retained for future investments, then the returns from those future investments must be at least as great as the dividends that could otherwise be declared in the present day, adjusted for time and risk. And, vice versa. This is saying that even retained earnings have a cost of capital, that being the opportunity cost of the value of the alternative use.

Capital in every form has at least one cost, that being the respective opportunity cost of doing something else with it that is potentially more gainful.

This is included as actual costs in the cash flows used for making important decisions, at least when done on a real economic basis and not only on an accounting basis (Bierman and Schmidt 2008). In a word, the cost of capital is the cost to the borrower, the corporation in this case, of getting investors to lend them their assets at all. In sum, think of the overall cost of capital as being the interest on bonds and the dividends on stock, which reflects the opportunity costs of other alternatives to the investor, considering the risks.

Introducing the Discount Rate and the Hurdle Rate

Some apportionment of the cost of capital, and usually a major apportionment, is included in the "hurdle rate" typically required of any capital project to meet in order to get approved and funded with precious investor capital. The cost of capital is at the heart of the capital project discount rate, but they are not always the same thing. A discount used for any immediate purpose may adjust the cost of capital for some good but unique reason, which is explained in detail in Volume II of this series.

Introducing Free Cash Flow

One of the most important parts of estimating the viability of any capital project is to determine the cash inflows and cash outflows. What makes it confusing is that there are different definitions and respective equations for calculating cash flow in the first place. Here, free cash flow (FCF) is most germane. Unfortunately, the imprecise use of terms that have precise definitions depending on the application, can lead to confusion. Of special interest here is that FCF has become popular at the corporate level:

(Smith and Hajric August 3, 2018).

... Chief Executive Officer Musk said late Wednesday he expects the company to generate positive free cash flow in the second half of this year, and become sustainably profitable for the first time in its 15-year history. He also said he expects to be able to use cash flow to repay around $900 million of convertible debt maturing early next year ...

"Sustained positive free cash flow will depend heavily on improving manufacturing efficiency and maintaining discipline on capital spending," [said an] S&P Global Ratings analyst.

Of course, that article speaks of the overall corporate perspective, and articles like that are ubiquitous. That noted, FCF is also something of a Holy Grail of capital project finance as well. But, the corporate concept and metric (a measure of overall corporate performance) differ from when the term is applied to specific capital projects (and as such, overall corporate FCF is not the simple sum of capital project FCFs).

This realization is critical to managing the distinction between a corporate portfolio of competencies (and divisions, or lines of business, or technologies) and managing a project portfolio of capital investments.

The term *cash flow* (lowercase) is first and foremost a general accounting idea, that idea being, to net the difference between cash inflows and outflows over a period of time. A common error is failing to express a *net* inflow-less-outflow but rather, only one or the other major term. For example, revenue is a cash *inflow*; netted costs, profit is *a* cash flow. At the top level of reporting, that is, on income statements by any name (e.g., cash flow statement, profit-and-loss statement), cash flow usually expresses revenue from sales less operating expenses, perhaps with some modification.

Budgets and Cash Flows: Operating versus Capital

The distinction between operating cash flow and FCF is also the basic distinction between operating projects (funded in the operating budget) and capital projects (funded in the capital budget, which together constitute the firm's overall master budget. See Volume II of this series.)

A point of interest, then, is how investments immediately affect the two main items in annual reports: income statements and balance sheets.

The investment-oriented expenses are separate from net income and are changes in accounts on the balance sheet: a change in fixed assets to reflect new fixed purchases and a change in net working capital, where net working capital is current assets minus current liabilities (Arnold and Nixon 2011, pp. 62–63)

Whereas

Operating Cash Flow =

(Revenues – Operating Expenses) (1 - Tax Rate)

+ Depreciation (Tax Rate)

+ Interest Expense (Tax Rate)

and

Capital Cash Flow or Cash Flow from Assets, CFA =

(Revenues – CGS and Selling, General and Admin) (1 - Tax Rate)

+ Depreciation (Tax Rate)

+ Interest Expense (Tax Rate)

– Change in Working Capital or (Current Assets – Current Liabilities)

– Change in Fixed Assets

FCF for capital projects

For an all-equity investment,

Free Cash Flow or FCF =

(Revenues – Operating Expenses) (1 - Tax Rate)

+ Depreciation (Tax Rate)

– Change in Net Working Capital

– Change in Fixed Assets

When fully explicated,

Free Cash Flow or FCF =

(Revenues – CGS and Selling, General and Admin) (1 - Tax Rate)

+ Depreciation (Tax Rate)

**– Change in Working Capital or (Current
Assets – Current Liabilities)**

– Change in Fixed Assets

That is a bit trickier than just saying that a project's cash flow is its revenues less its costs! Even at that level of understanding, this leads to a problem because no meaningful cash flows that occur over multiple periods such as in capital projects should ever be calculated without discounting. The equation does not contain a discounting factor!

Present Value and Discounted Cash Flow

Fortunately, the following equation combines both FCF and net present value, NPV:

Adjusted Present Value, APV =

$$\text{FCF} / (1 + k)^n + [(\text{Interest})\,(\text{Tax Rate})] / (1 + q)^n$$

For present purposes, to that point, a working knowledge of NPV and discounted cash flow (DCF) methods is assumed, as basic to the project executive's toolkit. The reader may first wish to consult with a corporate financier, or it is explained in Volume II of this series.

Conclusion

The purpose of this chapter was to frame upcoming chapters that more centrally focus on managing capital projects. By definition, capital projects directly allocate investment capital, where fiduciary responsibilities in the *C Suite* are directly linked to being attuned to shareholder concerns. In the modern view, corporations justify their costly organizational infrastructures and executive payrolls by developing portfolios of value-adding and hopefully synergistic, competencies, and capabilities. Later, discussions will operationalize this task in a mid-level project management organization, and explain. Despite some terminological confusion in terms like FCF, there is a necessary economic and financial link between capital project ROI, and overall corporate EVA, the economic profit that determines long-term corporate viability in the western capitalist tradition.

Discussion Questions

What is the difference between a single-business strategy and a corporate strategy? Can they ever be the same?

What does *competitive advantage* mean? How does this differ from your prior use (or abuse) of the term? How is it measured?

What is an investment? What are *returns* on an investment? How does that apply to capital projects?

Key Terms and Ideas

What is the strategic relevance of the distinction between a traditional *financial portfolio* and a modern *corporate portfolio* of *capabilities*? How is success measured?

What is *DCF, the discount rate, the hurdle rate, and FCF*? Use them to *connect the dots* between corporate and project management via *capital projects.*

CHAPTER 3

Capital Project Portfolios as Strategic Corporate Portfolios

Introduction

In any organization characterized by capital projects, some degree of formal coordination is likely to best serve the interests of all involved. Some dedicate and fund a separately organized effort to manage multiple projects as *portfolios*. Here, the Project Management Body of Knowledge (PMBOK) (2017) defines a *project management office (PMO) as "An organizational body or entity assigned various responsibilities related to the centralized and coordinated management of those projects under its domain."* In the project management vernacular, this applies especially to a *projectized* (PMI-PMBOK 2017) organization that uses the project management approach as a top-level organizing principle (a later discussion).

This applies to large and small organizations, especially the ones where there is a high level of capital and technology risk. There, a project portfolio is managed as a portfolio, that is, a unit with *unit* goals in addition to and apart from each *project-specific* goal set. The purpose of this chapter is to frame the PMO concept in the larger context of strategic corporate portfolios, introduced in the previous chapter.

After Studying this Chapter, the Reader will be Able to

Define PMO and explain some of the roles it can serve.

Explain how a capital project portfolio can also be a corporate portfolio of capabilities.

Discuss the purpose and contents of a business case used in the project proposal process.

Discuss the project appraisal process considering the pros and cons of the multicriteria assessment (MCA) method.

Give an example of how to map a capital project portfolio that would accomplish corporate goals.

The Project Management Organization

A PMO (PMI-PMBOK 2017) can be thought of as a mid-level point of management that exists at the juncture of executive management (including capital budgeting and capital rationing) and actual project sponsorship and management.

Managing capital projects as portfolios is analogous to managing multiple lines of business as portfolios of symbiotic, if not synergistic, competencies and capabilities, a mindset which usually outperforms corporations that are seen merely as portfolios of financial investments (Martinsuo and Killen 2014).

Killen, Hunt, Kleinschmidt et al. (2008) described a project portfolio management (PPM) capability:

> *PPM capabilities are a dynamic capability and a source of competitive advantage ... Managers can enhance and sustain competitive advantage by investing in tacit experience accumulation, explicit knowledge articulation, and explicit knowledge codification learning mechanisms to develop their PPM capability* (337).

First, it is one thing to *provide coordination* among projects that otherwise might not ever happen at all. If projects are seen as financial investments, for example, then composite project scheduling for the timing of overall cash flow generation can be very important (Sharifi and Safari 2016). This became obvious at Tesla, when the whole corporation became dangerously at risk of not having the revenues from the sales of earlier models, *just to be able to internally finance* the massive costs of scaling up for the Model 3.

Second, but less obvious, would be the kind of *knowledge management* needed to find a way to turn project-localized, *tacit learning* into a *corporate wide capability* with potential for *competitive advantage* (Teller, Kock and Gemunden 2015). *The previous chapter explained how important this is to modern thinking.* Recall that in its early years, Tesla chose to focus on its core competencies at battery-electric power trains, but in the same tactic, ignored opportunities to develop deep learning in the development of vehicles *from scratch* that its vision would certainly compel.

Third, an issue comes is the control of individual projects as well as coordination among them. It is again a matter of strategy, culture, and even executive style as to whether a PMO should be *pulling the strings* past project planning and say, then having very much to do with project execution, monitoring, and eventual close-out. Project managers should certainly have autonomy—but how much? As a matter of policy, it may not be enough to rely on a culture of having informal project *champions* running interference between project managers and *corporate.* Especially in organizations where the whole project management approach may be new, and a matrix form of organization still very immature, and where the simple reality is that most project managers are still inexperienced, some centralized guidance may be best.

Altogether, a PMO might guide the standardization of healthy "routines," but as well, consciously avoid turning them into pathological "rigidities." Finding the right balance is a key finding of almost 100 years of research in the management of innovation.

In other cases, it will be better for a PMO to only provide administrative support, say, for matters like the development of good and complete project proposals, *especially the finance sections!* The underlying exhibit compiles from several sources (Cleland and Ireland 2002; Kerzner 2006; PMI-PMBOK 2017) the possible roles and responsibilities for a PMO. This information is exhaustive and should be considered a menu of ideas.

Exhibit 3.1 Roles and Responsibilities of a PMO

Strategic support
    Executive support
        Develop project portfolio strategy
    Monitor the business environment
        Technology, product, industry lifecycles
    Knowledge management
        Tacit knowledge

Disseminate lessons learned
Codified knowledge
Policies, procedures, protocols
Intellectual property
Patents and trade secrets
Project coordination
Internal consulting
Formal stakeholder communications and documentation
Mentoring and training: Project finance
Develop quality standards
Continuous improvement
Benchmarking
Manage project interdependencies
Scheduling and resource conflicts
Alignment of goals
Develop standards
Best practices, processes, methods
Forms, checklists, templates
Project support
Planning
Project proposal development
Risk assessment: Facility planning
Execution, monitoring, and control
Status reporting: Earned value
Crisis management
Legal
Sign-off of deliverables
Compliance issues: Accounts and subcontractors
Formal closure
HR issues (especially under a matrix)
Post-project audits

It should be plain that a PMO can be many things, so certainly one should be tailored to the strategies and operational needs of any given organization.

Developing the Portfolio

This section assumes that a stable organizational structure and strategy are already in place, and that the organization is already acculturated to the project management philosophy and approach (see later chapter). These assumptions should not be taken lightly, however, as it can take years to develop any meaningful corporate culture. For a more complete treatment of this subject, the Project Management Institute publishes a separate ANSI standard—in the list of references, see PMI-Competency (2017). As well, the reader is invited to browse other standards and publications related to this series at www.pmi.org.

Project Proposals

In the project management literature, there is no shortage of advice about how to write project proposals, but a few extra words should help frame the task for capital projects.

Any capital project proposal should articulate how financial returns will accrue to the investors of capital, especially stockholders ("the owners") and bond creditors (see Volume II).

Experienced project managers know that writing a good proposal is not very different from the task of any independent entrepreneur writing a business plan, in order to get financing from any institution—even the local family-owned commercial bank of Mom 'n' Pop. And then, acquiring real venture capital, that is, private capital, is another world entirely. This discussion assumes the publicly traded, that is, post-initial public offering (post-IPO) world, the more typical world of corporate financiers. In that world, a term often heard is business case. In short, the kind of proposal needed to gain approval is similar to a business plan, with common-sense modifications.

The task is to get financing from managers of capital, which means positive financial "returns." It is also an exercise of due diligence for managers with fiduciary responsibilities.

As adapted for present purposes, a thorough example of a business case appears as follows (Cohen and Graham 2001; Heerkens 2006; Hisrich 1998).

Exhibit 3.2 Business Case format

1.0 Front matter

   1.1 Cover sheet

      1.1.1 Title

      1.1.2 Author and organization

      1.1.3 Contributor(s) and organization

      1.1.4 Current date

   1.2 Document control

      1.2.1 Version number

      1.2.2 Version history

   1.3 Review/approval table

   1.4 Table of contents

2.0 Executive summary

   2.1 Description of business needs

   2.2 Strategic linkages

   2.3 Summary of options considered

   2.4 Preferred option(s) and justification

   2.5 *Summary of financial analysis*

   2.6 Inaction risks

   2.7 Key recommendations

3.0 The business case

   3.1 Business case subject

   3.2 Business case purpose

   3.3 Intended audience

   3.4 Analytical methodology

      3.4.1 Scope and boundaries

      3.4.2 *Financial metrics*

      3.4.3 Data sources and methods

   3.5 Disclaimer

4.0 Situational assessment

   4.1 Description of the problem, need, or opportunity

      4.1.1 Background and current situation

      4.1.2 Gap statement: Current versus desired situations

      4.1.3 Stakeholders and their interests

4.2 Investment goals

    4.2.1 Business outcomes and results

    4.2.2 Business benefits and key value drivers

4.3 Strategic alignment

    4.3.1 Strategic relationships

    4.3.2 Integration considerations

    4.3.3 Position relative to other initiatives

4.4 Situational analysis (product or service)

    4.4.1 Market analysis

    4.4.2 Customer or user analysis

    4.4.3 Competitor analysis

    4.4.4 Gap analysis, product (current versus desired)

4.5 Situational analysis: Process

    4.5.1 Process(es) affected

    4.5.2 Existing process model

    4.5.3 Desired process model

    4.5.4 Gap analysis, process (current versus desired)

4.6 Critical success factors

4.7 Completion criteria

5.0 Alternatives assessment

  5.1 *Description of feasible alternatives*

  5.2 Comparison of alternatives

    5.2.1 Scope and boundaries

    5.2.2 Results and effects

    5.2.3 Advantages and disadvantages

    5.2.4 Organizational and stakeholder impacts

    5.2.5 Implementation and integration considerations

  5.3 *Analytical framework*

    5.3.1 *Cost model*

    5.3.2 *Benefits model*

  5.4 *Financial (quantitative) analysis*

    5.4.1 *Cash outflows (items of cash)*

    5.4.2 *Cash inflows (financial benefits)*

    5.4.3 *Cash flow chart*

    5.4.4 *Cash flow analysis*

5.5 *Comprehensive (qualitative) analysis*
    5.5.1 *Qualitative benefits rationale*
    5.5.2 *Weighted factor scoring matrix*
5.6 *Finance and accounting effects*
5.7 Summarization of initial alternatives assessment
6.0 *Risk and sensitivity analysis*
    6.1 *Key risk factors*
    6.2 *Risk quantification and probability distributions*
    6.3 *Probabilistic risk analysis*
    6.4 *Potential problem analysis (qualitative)*
    6.5 *Best-case or worst-case analysis*
    6.6 *Mitigation strategies*
    6.7 *Interpretation of risk assessment*
    6.8 *Preferred alternative*
7.0 *Contingencies and dependencies*
    7.1 *Value chain analysis*
    7.2 *Product and process*
    7.3 *Functional and operational*
    7.4 *Procedural*
    7.5 Summary and key responsibilities
8.0 Implementation strategies and action planning
    8.1 Preferred alternatives: Scope
    8.2 Enabling implementation activities
        8.2.1 *Product development activities*
        8.2.2 *Process development activities*
        8.2.3 *Capital improvements*
        8.2.4 Product and process certifications
    8.3 *Funding strategies*
    8.4 Project management strategies
        8.4.1 Project governance model
        8.4.2 Resource requirements
        8.4.3 Execution methods
        8.4.4 Procurement and acquisition methods
        8.4.5 Implementation timeline

8.5 Key Deliverables and results
8.6 Verification of deliverables and results
8.7 Transition considerations
8.8 Management model, post-project
9.0 Summary, conclusions, and recommendations

Appraising Project Proposals

Moving to the consideration of which projects to choose, each firm should have a process like this (Baker and English 2011):

1. ***Identify project proposals.*** This is a preliminary screening, often done bottom-up, and involves the creation of several business cases by hopeful project sponsors.
2. ***Estimate project and cash flows.*** *These should be incremental, after-tax cash flows. The key term of interest "free cash flow," explained earlier.*
3. ***Evaluate projects.*** *Establish the financial viability of each project using a method that "discounts" the cash flows. Qualitative measures will also affect any decision.*
4. ***Select projects.*** This is a good time just to mention the impact that psychology has on the process (later discussions expound at length). For example, decision-makers should "… avoid investment in low-return projects that occurs when managers have private information and incentives for controlling more assets and managerial understatement of current performance in order to lower their future performance targets" (Baker and English 2011, p. 2). Said more academically, project sponsors experience *agency problems* that can bias their proposals. It is not always intentional; *opportunistic* behaviors are a matter of misaligned incentives. Similar *human* problems are discussed from the *economics* point of view later.
5. ***Implement projects.*** Global best practices point to guidance from organizations like the Project Management Institute, summarized in a later chapter.

6. ***Perform post-completion audit.*** This can affect the institution-alization of *tacit knowledge* as well as the codification of what can be recorded for others to learn from. The disparity from potential to practice is unfortunate, because building *capabilities* is directly affected.

Multicriteria Project Assessment

Whether a project is being considered as a standalone option or part of a portfolio of related options, an additional tool worth considering is known as multicriteria assessment, MCA. MCA is a general management technique not exclusive to project management. It is flexible, and its ben-efits derive largely from developing and tailoring the right tool, because that alone helps develop strategic thinking and aids management com-munication. The effort put into the development of the tool is just as important as its application. Here, it is being suggested that MCA can be useful when developing strategic project portfolios. The approach is an attempt to rationalize complex, *apples and oranges* decisions, but is not recommended here as replacing executive judgment. MCA should aid it.

To frame the kind of problems MCA is well-suited for, consider, with hints in italics:

(Ferris November 2, 2017).

"… we can see scenarios in which [Tesla] is able to overcome tem-porary production challenges, manage distribution/service challenges, execute on growth, achieve aggressive margin targets, and build a cash generative/self-sustaining growth engine (if Tesla's production and margin targets are achieved, the company could reach [Free Cash Flow] breakeven by late-2018) … However … we believe that the margin for error is once again becoming uncomfortably thin."

That excerpt is so intimidating, it becomes sardonically funny. Though all the measures were applied to Tesla on the whole, it all came down to success or failure on the Model 3, which can easily be imagined as a port-folio of synergistic capital projects. More simply, recall the days when the

Roadster *was* the whole company, and the whole *bet the company* project portfolio. The semi could also serve as example, or for that matter, the entire bevy of solar products. In any event, the point is that once new product development (by any name) achieves *projectized* success, *normal* operations might resume.

As the article makes urgent, several criteria should sometimes be used to evaluate any capital project proposal, especially when developing portfolios with superordinate goals that demand so-called *synergies*. (The term often ignores more rigorous economics.) Sometimes, the goals are not easy to reconcile; indeed, sometimes, they oppose each other, and decisions can become stressed. Not only is it necessary to simultaneously consider free cash flow and other financial metrics, it is often necessary to consider non-financial qualitative variables (e.g., regulatory compliance, community image, and in Tesla's case, political opposition) that do not lend themselves to easy measurement.

The obvious problem, of course, is that this creates *apples and oranges* dilemmas. But, *soft* measures do matter and should be considered as an equal part of the formal process—that is, not just by arbitrary, *ad hoc*, and personally biased afterthoughts and impulses. Recalling the public relations problems that Musk personally created for himself and the company, readers should take note. The picture being painted is a caricature just to make a point, but in any event, it might be best for legal reasons alone to institutionalize and document judgment to some degree.

Advantages "… include ease and use, its understanding and acceptance within an organization, perceived usefulness, and the time and cost of implementation." Disadvantages are that

> … leaders need to be involved at the different organizational levels to ensure that incentives exist for managers to adopt the new system and to encourage their interest and participation. *Relevant executives of a company need to formulate or agree on the set of criteria to use that corresponds with the values and goals of the corporation and the related weights assigned* (Fernholz 2011, p. 467).

It should go without saying that the sooner, the better.

That point is important enough to dwell on for a moment. Research generally finds that while plans have limited use, the planning *process* is worth the effort even if, as they saying goes, the plan itself is thrown out. *Planning alone forces managers to communicate, air their assumptions, if not their differences of opinion, and hopefully reconcile them.* Planning should get everybody who will be involved later in the *execution* stage *on the same page* when there is still time and opportunity to preclude nasty surprises. Managers become coordinated at the outset and aware of how their roles interact and mutually depend. Another positive result is a stronger culture at the executive level. Speculation will be left up to the reader, but Musk's autocratic management style—not always to good effect—is well-documented.

Recall that Musk once said, literally, "we were idiots" with reference to scaling up the *dreadnought* Fremont factory. He was thinking of failures made in the design phase, that is, to not consider *manufacturability* as a *design parameter* from the outset. After all, at the Fremont facility robots were hung from the ceiling, an entire team was flown in from Germany to fix things, parts were made by hand, and a makeshift tent was needed to make Model 3s next to the main building. Had *manufacturability* (or derivative metrics) been included as part of the capital project planning process—who knows?

Anyway, the more precise issue about planning concerns MCA for capital projects.

> As the transparency of the MCA process increases for the team involved, so does the quality of the output, advice, decision making, and even implementation that emerges from the system. Transparency itself may be another challenge, depending on corporate culture and context (Fernholz 2011, pp. 478–479).

The way to go about it is identical in principle to any weighted sum approach: individual decision criteria are determined, then they are assigned weights, and an overall index is created. In other words, each criterion's measurement is multiplied by the assigned weight, and weights are added. First, then, preliminary discussions lead to agreement (or at least consensus) about which dimensions should be used as the decision criteria. Then, each is assigned a weight that represents its importance relative to the other criteria (which automatically results in an ordinal prioritization as well). When used to evaluate a project, each criterion is assigned a project-specific score on a common scale, whether numerical or categorical—this is where an unavoidable apples-to-oranges problem happens, if it has not happened already.

In any event, each criterion contributes in a proportional way to an overall view where again, each is assigned some qualitative or quantitative weight and computed like any weighted factoring method.

There is no one way to go about any of this, so table 3.1 is presented merely to be suggestive. This is not to exclude the need to include such factors as marketing and sales, human resources, *and the interests of the keenest external stakeholders*:

Table 3.1 MCA *scoring factors and targets*

Strategic	Operational	Financial
Contribution to economic value-added (EVA) (Estimate beyond "profit")	Economies of scale and scope (Unit cost versus pricing)	Cost of capital (e.g., capital structure policy)
Capability/competence (Competitive advantage)	Real options analysis (e.g., learning effects)	Hurdle rate (WACC, CAPM beta, RADR)
Vertical integration (Supply chain collaboration)	Horizontal integration (Capacity, breakeven)	NPV (Profitability index as ROI)
Market necessity (e.g., share)	Logistics (e.g., service points)	IRR (Ranking)
Non-market necessity (e.g., legal)	Governance (e.g., Wall Street)	Payback (Liquidity, free cash flow)

Research in the matter indicates varied results, but one can deduce several benefits from the following description:

> [D]ecision makers can use MCA methods ... by gradually incorporating more information and ... by reviewing regularly the weights after realizing the results of previous decisions. The consistency of the results tends to increase through time ... organizations

are observed to improve performance in decision making and in subsequent phases of the capital budgeting cycle (Fernholz 2011, p. 475).

Covering the Total Innovation Cycle

One classic depiction of a project portfolio is reproduced as Table 3.2 (Clark and Wheelwright 2002). *The table dimensionalizes technological innovations into two types: product and process. This is typical strategic thinking as technology evolves through product and industry lifecycles.* Related, business strategy is all about establishing and sustaining competitive advantage, and theory asserts that there are two generic types of advantage: low cost and differentiation. Early in the evolution of technology, product, and industry lifecycles, product technology innovations focus attention on performance or differentiation more so than the price or cost. As lifecycles evolve, differentiation advantage tends to give way to low-cost-based strategies and process innovation.

Therefore, the table intrinsically invites an evolutionary perspective. Trends in the table can be roughly surmised to flow stepwise, first top-to-bottom and then left-to-right. Early in cycles, new or core product innovations are made, followed by new or core process innovations as their immediate consequence. At the opposite corner, incremental, *derivative* innovations of both types happen. From there, the intrigue gravitates to the middle word *platform*, which appeared many times in the media as an important part of electric vehicle (EV) design approaches (McGrath 1996; Schilling 2005; Mohr, Sengupta and Slater 2005; Narayanan 2000).

Table 3.2 Capital project portfolio

		Process			
		New or core	Next-gen	Upgrade	Incremental
Product	New or core	Radical			
	Next-gen		Platform	Platform	Platform
	Family		Platform	Derivative	Derivative
	Incremental		Platform	Derivative	Derivative

Even without modification, this classic matrix can be used as the basis of a capital project portfolio. It combines the major types of innovation into an evolutionary strategy, considering product and process innovations, radical-through-incremental, over the technology and industry lifecycle. It suggests a steady state that sustains itself, and as such, it suggests the logic of a portfolio of capabilities as well as a portfolio of capital investments.

More About the Industry Lifecycle

One of the most enduring management frameworks has been the industry lifecycle (ILC), an *economics* model that extends what in *marketing* is called the product lifecycle (PLC). An ILC subsumes all the PLCs that happen in an industry over a long period (Abernathy and J.M. Utterback 1988; Grant 2002; Mohr, Sengupta and Slater 2005; Narayanan 2000; Porter 1980; Schilling 2005; Tidd, Bessant and Pavitt 2001). A point of confusion is that the PLC and ILC are both defined by the same four phases: introduction, growth, maturity, and decline. Otherwise, they are not the same thing and should not be confused.

Academia has always assumed that the ILC begins when the introduction phase begins, that is, once a new product is made available for purchase. The ILC does not consider pre-commercialization activity, so here, a new product development (NPD) *phase* is assumed. See the underlying table (adapted from McGrath 2012).

In many industries, much research and development (R&D) work is first performed for decades by universities, non-profit consortia, venture capitalists, secretive corporations with *deep pockets*, backyard crackpots, and all sorts of entrepreneurs in between. By the time consumers become aware that a *technological breakthrough* has been made in such-and-such, sometimes, decades of slow scientific and engineering research—painstaking, sometimes useless, and punctuated by fits and starts—has occurred. Certainly, this applies to EVs and Tesla. Otherwise, the EV story showed characteristics of different ILC phases at once. In the grand sweep of things, product technology was still early in the cycle, and the prevailing production paradigm was undergoing a massive period of rejuvenation. Technology was at both ends of the cycle—in a way.

Table 3.3 Modified ILC

	NPD "EV": Tesla	Introduction	Growth	Maturity "auto": Incumbents	Decline (or rejuvenation)
Profitability, measured as average firm profit	Bleeding cash—no revenues	Negative—unit costs still exceed unit revenues	Turns positive, possibly lucrative margins	Positive, but shows slim margins at high volumes	Problematic, firms fail and exit
Key competencies and success factors	NPD	Technology Sell sizzle to technophiles Product innovation Establish image	Marketing Technology standards Dominant design Build supply chains Transition from/to innovation types	Operations Low cost Design for "X" Price sensitivity Hard to differentiate Standardization at high quality	Finance Commit to loyal customers Rationalization, cost-cutting
Demand	N/A	Early adopters	Market penetration	Price-sensitive mass market Repeat business	Obsolescence
Technology	Lab	Rapid innovation among incompatible designs	Dominant design emerges Emphasis from product to process innovation	Diffused, well-known Difficulty maintaining appropriability	Little innovation
Products	Prototypes	Poor quality Rapid advances	Encroaching dominant design	Commoditization and low cost plus niches of differentiation	Focused on remaining customer needs
Manufacturing and supply chain	Ad hoc	Short runs, specialized labor, labor-intense Specialized channels Direct sales	Shifting to mass production Competition to dominate key channels From institutions to retail	Overcapacity, capital-intense, de-skilled labor, long runs Supply chains compete Mass merchandizing	Chronic overcapacity Highly selective customer base
Competition	N/A	Few and disparate	Rapid entry, rapid exit, mergers, and so on	Many until price wars Survivors are similar in most ways	Strategic withdrawals

In another important way, the EV industry *was in the growth stage—not only in terms of* firm-specific profits, *but* structural, economic profitability *across the board. This is a key to understanding much of the Tesla controversy,* that is, *this is not "just semantics!"*

Note how the whole EV story in the media was rife with the word *profitability*, but normally used the word with reference to a company or even a product like the Model 3. In the truest strategic sense, the word profitability best applies to an industry on the whole, then it applies to where a firm is positioned in that context.

In the ILC, one thing that separates introduction from growth is not only *faster* growth, but *accelerating* growth in the total sales by all industry players combined. It is the rate as well as the total that matters. Rising aggregate industry sales means rising cumulative production and generally, falling average unit costs.

Low unit prices that do not meet unit production costs can be part of a viable strategy when market penetration is the strategic intent. This is especially valid where markets are new. There is also nothing wrong with postponing profits if rapid expansion, even *at a loss*, means establishing a first mover advantage, that is, precluding others from doing something similar.

Different strategies will normally result in early profits for some firms, but not all. Most particularly, firms that have *priced low* or even *lowballed* from the outset are positioned to see early profits—but not to achieve true profitability. An industry helps establish its own *legitimacy* when the *average* firm-specific profit becomes positive (Porter 1980; Besanko, Dranove and Shanley 2000; Tirole 1990). Economists look at this as an important milestone. When *average* industry profitability turns positive to stay (*structurally*), potential new entrants see this as a signal to enter and no longer sit on the sidelines, that is, they stop being spectators. Until that point, if a new industry, on average, loses money, wasting precious investment capital, there is a possibility that the industry will not survive. Hope may spring eternal for technology enthusiasts and environmentalists, but it does not on *Wall Street*.

Internal Corporate Venturing

Consider:

(Frost January 5, 2018).

... in the latest move by major carmakers to adapt to rapid industry change by investing in startups through their own venture capital arms...

... many are investing directly in the new services - and gaining access to intellectual property - via their own corporate venture capital (CVC) funds.

CVC funds, a familiar feature of innovative sectors ... let companies skip some of the formalities otherwise required for new investments, and pounce more swiftly on promising startups.

This excerpt illustrates what in the technology and innovation management literature is generally called internal corporate venturing, ICV (Burgelman and Sayles 1986). The term is fairly self-explanatory, and here will be taken to mean any separately organized effort within any *bureaucratic* organization, with hopes of manifesting the myths ordinarily expected only of small dynamic start-ups, also with overtones about the typical goals of venture capital. *The overriding goal is the development of a new innovative competency that later can be parlayed into a more broad-based corporate capability* (Block and MacMillan 1995; Rothwell and Dodgson 1994; Tidd, Bessant, and Pavitt 2001). ICV projects are necessarily collaborative with outsiders, but the general toolkit is that of the project manager (Kerzner 2009). Consider the following excerpt, which is a textbook vignette full of key terms and ideas. Italics are added:

(Rosevear April 08, 2017).

General Motors is running its self-driving car program like a *start-up*, ... Cruise is now a GM *subsidiary;* Cruise's CEO ... has "full responsibility for the operational and financial performance of our autonomous vehicle business" ...

Cruise will be the *business center* ... GM may report its earnings results as a *separate business segment* ... ...Cruise Automation -- has a budget. They have short- and long-term financial targets, and it's monitored at the highest levels of the organization ...

... GM's self-driving effort is getting close to leaving the lab and becoming a business reality -- and GM is aiming to show that it's not about to be "disrupted" by new technology companies.

In the preceding excerpt, one large incumbent was trying to co-opt, if not appropriate, innovation *routines*. Similar attempts in the industry would likely have a spotty record across the board and over time. An ICV approach might save the day at any given instance. The goal of the ICV is not to abandon the past outright, but to combine the valuable resources of a corporation with the benefits of a small and more entrepreneurial one. This should not be attempted too suddenly. The new venture would pose a higher risk-return profile than what is traditional for the organization, but not an irrationally high one either.

The ICV approach would be close to that of a venture capitalist, not a person that no investor would ever venture to capitalize.

An ICV seeks to (Tidd, Bessant and Pavitt 2001):

- *learn core competencies from other organizations;*
- *change the competencies and culture within an existing organization; and*
- *develop a separate organization within itself and importantly, one with a different structure, set of processes, and culture.*

An ICV is a serious formal endeavor—not an informal insurgence—and not to be taken lightly at any level of management. The inherent risks and uncertainties demand flexibility and a certain instinct, but not at the cost of managerial accountability. Managers need to consider how the organization will fit into its particular environment.

In his days, famed economist Joseph Schumpeter worried that large corporations would eventually learn to appropriate entrepreneurial processes and routines, if not to adopt that kind of culture entirely.

Table 3.4 Internal corporate venture options

	Base technology	**Related technology**	**Unrelated technology**
Base market	Internal development	Internal development	Joint venture
Related market	Internal development	*Internal corporate venture*	*Internal corporate venture*
Unrelated market	Joint venture	*Internal corporate venture*	Acquisition (or merger)

Deciding on the organizational structure and size begins by thinking in terms of two dimensions: the relatedness of the new venture's technology-competence-capability to existing ones and how similar the targeted market relates to the ones already being served. See Table 3.4; it considers a very broad range of situations.

In Table 3.4, *internal development* is appropriate when the firm basically knows what it is doing, and what it is up against. The goal is to continuously improve the existing and successful combination of capability, market savvy, and existing technology. One can assume relatively incremental improvements here, but the real point for the moment is the lack of external collaboration. Costs of development and risks are low, but so is the expected return on investment. However, the term *business as usual* is not right because the endgame is organizational innovation, not product innovation *per se*. Given the modesty of the effort, of course, this approach can stop short of making sure that its results permeate the entire organization. New *capabilities* development—not NPD right at the moment—can take very long or not really happen fully.

At the opposite corner of the table, there is outright *Acquisition*. The main advantages and disadvantages here are the inverse of internal development: it is faster, but generally costlier, and several kinds of risk are high. The economically correct cost of an acquired outfit is a true financial management challenge. In terms of risks, though, not all are financial. A major cause of failure in such moves is cultural incompatibility, and many managers fail to consider how important it will be for them, *personally*, to see to the transition. Otherwise, the bally-hood synergies may never happen. Relatedly, a true *joint venture* creates a new legal entity, one formed by the combined investment of two or more firms, possibly with the intention of an initial public offering (IPO). Thus, the intention assumes a great degree of autonomy, independence, and responsibility for results. One possibility fully intended from the start is *spin off*—selling the unit to the highest bidder when the opportunity is right.

Between these corners is the ICV. The idea is to find an optimum, an organizational hybrid of a kind, between the advantages and disadvantages of the previous choices. ICV assumes some degree of involvement of at least one other outside firm, as opposed to strictly confined internal development—but not full ownership and control.

More About External Collaboration

When considering options for how to collaborate with other firms for reasons that include technology development, there are whole categories of distinctly different choices. See Table 3.5, which complements and amplifies the aforementioned discussion (Blois 1996; Buckley and Casson 1996; Mariti and Smiley 1996; Tidd, Bessant, and Pavitt 2001).

Most of the decisions implied in the table are done on the initiative of the buyer. Licensing, however, usually goes the other way—a patent-holder often takes the initiative and markets a patent for licensing; just as possibly for outright sale, rights, and all. Conversely, the buyer firm may be so interested in a patent and its founder, who they will sometimes acquire (*buyout*) the entire firm. This often happens when a large incumbent is on a drive to acquire a technology quickly.

A franchise is a complicated licensing arrangement, a legal form of organization with rules and regulations all its own. The basic idea in a franchise is that access to (usually process) technology is exchanged for royalties to its production. The idea extends far beyond fast-food and small retail.

To a large degree, consortia happen during pre-commercialization efforts. Often, participation is led by universities, public science-based institutions, or sundry not-for-profit researchers. Despite the appeal of for largesse and collegiality, though, there are proprietary and appropriability issues.

A true strategic alliance occurs among firms that are competitors, but have common goals concerning non-strategic or at least non-competitive issues. For example, this happens when safety concerns exist, especially when it is in each firm's interest to cooperate for the good of the (possibly new and tenuous) industry. Otherwise, in business jargon, the term is usually used loosely.

A joint venture between two firms creates a third, stock issuing public company, with the founders usually being main investors. Whereas a merger or acquisition (as in *M&A*) more simply means the outright purchase of one firm by another, often using stock as the exchange currency.

The sloppy word partnership (lowercase) can mean just about anything. Uppercase, though, it refers to a legal form of ownership that is the same as sole proprietorship, except that there are several equal owners, and principals share all rights and responsibilities. Most are small businesses, but some are amazingly huge; there is no legal limit. Another formal use of the term is entirely different—a general partner refers to

Table 3.5 Collaboration options

Relationship	Remarks
Licensing	Common choice for simple technology transfer; practically, an extension of patent law and policy. The clarity and completion of the agreement determines moral hazard and inherent opportunism.
Franchise	Similar to a complex license, a legal form of organization that trades access to production technology and brand capital, for a cut of the proceeds (e.g., royalties).
Consortium	Generally seen when a technology still shows very uncertain profitability, for example, is too complex or technically difficult for any one firm to see a clear internal path to commercialization.
Alliance	Firms that normally compete in markets for sales revenues, but have non-competitive interests in common. When goals are reached, the alliance may be due for dissolution.
Joint venture	Assuming two principals, creates a third legal entity co-owned (through stock stock) by the founding firms. Often experience mismanaged and ruinous organizational culture clashes.
Network	Not a legal form of business. Practically unplannable, fluid, and responsive, but highly vulnerable to opportunism among the players, especially as people transfer among firms.
Partnership	Very commonly abused term; usually has no legal meaning or is not well-defined. When a legal form of business, just like sole proprietorship but with several co-founders and co-owners. Also used in the venture capital context as a general partnership.

one entity in a venture capital relationship. Otherwise, *partnership* is just a common expression.

Finally, a network is as much of a socio economic phenomenon as it is planned and organized. A network may include any or every legal form of organization, or none. There may not be many contracts, because networks depend on personal initiative and informal social habits, that is, *who you know*. Silicon Valley is the quintessential model, but there is no legal definition.

Conclusion

The main purpose of this chapter was to extend the discussion of the previous chapter, assuming a change in audience from the corporate executive to the capital project manager, especially where the two levels interface. Specifically, the well-developed concept of a project portfolio, managed by a standing and dedicated PMO, was described as operationalizing the strategic idea of a corporate portfolio of value-adding competencies and capabilities. Two classic examples helped illustrate.

Discussion Questions

What are some of the pros and cons of a formal PMO?

What are some contributions that a PMO can make in developing and sustaining a corporate portfolio of capabilities?

What comprises the purpose and contents of a business case used in the project proposal process?

Exercises

Construct an MCA to evaluate projects in any organization of your choice.

Map out a capital project portfolio for any organization of your choice.

CHAPTER 4

Communication and Stakeholder Management

Introduction

The story of Tesla's brief life through 2018 made clear that there were some communication and stakeholder issues worth discussing. There they were presented much as they were in the business media, largely for the sake of investor interest. Of course, the list of stakeholders in the Tesla saga is more extensive than that, at least including environmentalists, employees, suppliers, regular *car guys*, and more. Most had legitimate interests, that is, this was no soap opera to them.

This chapter focuses on the management of project communication and project stakeholder interests. These two areas of interest are, individually, *knowledge areas* in the Project Management Institute's paradigm of thought leadership in the area. The next chapter outlines that paradigm. Because these two areas were so acute in the Tesla story, a separate chapter has been given them here, especially toward executive interest in capital project finance.

After Studying this Chapter, the Reader will be Able to

Explain how formal methods and processes can be used by executives to communicate effectively with external stakeholders.

Compare and contrast a private investor environment with a post-initial public offering (post-IPO) one, focusing on the fiduciary responsibilities of executives.

Define corporate governance and provide examples of pitfalls from the research evidence, and contrast group phenomena from individual effects.

Define and briefly explain the practical relevance of these terms: principle–agent relationship, information asymmetry, and moral hazard.

Explain several ways how managerial biases in capital project decision-making processes can affect the cost of capital and project discount or hurdle rates.

Executive Communication in Capital Project Environments

The Tesla experience shows how important it is for managers of corporate capital, including many capital project managers, to consider communications issues seriously (Collyer 2017; Eskerod, Huemann and Ringhofer 2016; Eskerod, Huemann and Savage 2016; Muller, Turner, Andersen, Shao and Kvalnes 2017). Though many technology-oriented people eschew such problems as *common sense* and not in need of much formal direction, the opposite is sometime the case. To illustrate, it is one thing to observe how Elon Musk's methods of touching base with his benefactors were not only strained, but also elicited a move to have him ousted from one executive role, and even got him personally indicted by the Securities and Exchange Commission (SEC). That is so glaringly obvious and speaks so strongly to personality, the story might seem anomalous. However, it is another thing to dismiss it too quickly and think that managing the issues cannot be improved. It is simply not the case that common sense is as common as one thinks. Consider:

> **(Mukherjee May 3, 2018).**
>
> ... Musk refused to answer questions from analysts on Tesla's capital requirements, saying "boring questions are not cool" ...
>
> Morgan Stanley's [official] said it was the most unusual he had heard in 20 years in the business, noting that "the analysts on the call represent the providers of capital that Tesla has throughout its history depended upon" ...
>
> ... a Los Angeles-based private equity firm, called it "the single greatest CEO meltdown in American car history."

Just when it looked like things had calmed down after a few months had passed, one small slip multiplied the damage several times over:

(Hunnicut August 30, 2018).

… Some corporate governance activists call for the chairman and CEO roles to be split between two people to improve oversight …

Musk has been under pressure over the company's spending and after tweeting on Aug. 7 that he planned to take the company private, only to abandon the idea by Aug. 24 …

"BlackRock's approach to investment stewardship is driven by our fiduciary duties to our clients, the asset owners … Our approach to engaging with companies and proxy voting activities is consistent with our commitment to drive long term shareholder value for our clients."

Most executives are not like Elon Musk, and the aforementioned issues were not project-specific, but the point about the importance of communication remains the same—made especially acute here as it relates not only to project success, but also to corporate governance on the whole. Communications management is a vital element in overall stakeholder management when large amounts of investment capital are at risk. Especially, when large institutions become the major owners of a firm, as opposed to a widely distributed ownership among countless *retail investors*, each one becomes a credible voice and force in corporate governance.

As time goes on, corporate ownership (equity) is becoming more and more concentrated and institutional; combined with a trend toward greater activism, these points will only become truer over time.

Of course, internal communications are botched all the time, too. An abundance of evidence supports the assertion that categorically speaking, *soft* factors like poor communications plans, policies, and procedures are the most common causes of project failure (Cleland and Ireland 2002; Kerzner 2006; Meredith and Mantel 2009). But, soft does not necessarily mean informal.

An important principle in Weber's original theory of bureaucracy (Wren 2007) is that managers are beholden first and foremost to the expectations of their offices, and formal communications should express that. By "formal," it is usually meant official, usually written, perhaps legally binding, as well as obedient to standing organizational rules.

In its treatment of project communications management, the Project Management Body of Knowledge Guide (PMBOK) emphasizes *formal* communication issues, in part as a matter of formal documentation. As an obvious example, an overall project plan should contain a separate section that addresses formal communications for purposes of assuring contractual compliance, conflict resolution procedures, and *paper trails* if nothing else. Beyond documentation for archival reasons, the plan should specify who gets what information, when, and by what medium. Even if project documentation suggested in the PMBOK is never used operationally, it is not done merely for posterity. These days, of course, it is not uncommon for specific projects to have their own websites, at least for local consumption. Electronic media offer an incredible array of options, so the real *body of knowledge* is always a work in progress. But, the point seems timeless.

"Bureaucracy" can be of great use if understood and managed properly, even in innovative cultures. Joseph Schumpeter, the guru of "creative destruction" and "entrepreneurship," insisted on this many decades ago, but nobody seems to have noticed.

Contrary to the popular belief, Schumpeter's championship of entrepreneurship was not unequivocal. He saw, almost 100 years ago now, that even very large and old organizations can learn to be innovative and at least keep pace with the *small guys*. In the author's favorite words, *innovation processes are now routine*, though, by definition, they are and cannot become *routinely successful*. Project management practices are case in point.

Corporate Governance of Investor Capital

When the word *governance* is used in the corporate context, it includes the forces that compel managers to maintain their fiduciary responsibilities to the owners of invested equity, bond creditors, and the like. Of course, there are many disparate forms of governance that represent all the various *stakeholder* groups, not just *stockholders*. The full list of executive responsibilities goes beyond fiduciary duties alone, but that is the focus for now. Given the present focus, then, it should be understood how *going public* changes a firm from the standpoint of investor expectations and interests.

An IPO's Impact on Corporate Orientation

When Tesla *went public* in 2010, it meant that it became approved by the U.S. SEC to sell shares of stock on exchanges such as the New York Stock Exchange (NYSE), which sits among other stock exchanges all around the world in major centers of finance such as London, Hong Kong, and Tokyo. The process is called issuing an IPO. The *offer* is one of selling stock to the general public on an exchange. At that point, the corporation is said to be publicly owned or publicly traded.

On pre-IPO financing, *private capital* is almost synonymous with the term venture capital—except that field also includes the art of making leveraged buyouts (LBOs) of often-desperate firms, sometimes more pejoratively called vulture capital. The two strains of interest should not be confused, but private capital includes both financial arms under the one term.

That clarified, an important related term is *angel investor*. By bringing in the kinds of personal funds, it would take to keep a young company afloat, and usually motivated by a super-ordinate concern like saving the planet, for example, Musk was very typical of the classic angel investor—except the term usually refers to strong (and usually rich) believers who provide funds, but then stay out of the way. There is no formal definition, but, obviously, Musk was not an angel in this sense, and given his personality and style, it is difficult to imagine him not wanting active participation in return for the risks he took with his own money.

Also, Elon Musk was the major owner or stockholder of Tesla throughout the period being considered. Placing their money where their mouths were, the stated ambitions of Tesla founders did not include cashing out and getting rich quick(ly). Their stated ambitions were long term and lofty and foretold *with a degree of certainty* the ongoing re-investment of most of their potential personal gain, as well as the capital of external investors.

It is a matter of financial strategy as to what to do about publicly traded equity after an IPO, and in what combination this is done with issuing debt (i.e., selling corporate bonds). The point is that there are many options about what to do if-and-when a firm *goes public*. Still, in a basic sense, Tesla's story was rather typical of how an IPO usually breaks a young enterprise from private capital sources of funding.

The next point, though, is that there is indeed a big difference between the expectations of pre-IPO investors and their associated risks, rewards, and entire sets of motives, compared to post-IPO investors. As one should expect, past an IPO, the expectations of investors can change suddenly, and in fact, usually that is why most private capital is withdrawn according to plan. It is typical, for example, for a venture capitalist to hold an expectation of a 20 percent return in only five years (prior to IPO), while the general public normally has much more modest expectations and different time horizons.

Again, IPOs have a reputation for making *instant* millionaires of most of an upper management echelon, and sometimes, this seems to be the main reason for taking the plunge, that is, for *selling out* to the highest bidder. It is not uncommon for a technology entrepreneur to have these goals in mind all along. Ironically, the Tesla team was patient about getting rich or at least, apparently more so than about saving the planet. They could have cashed out very young, very rich, and would have been well-justified for doing so.

With that in mind, consider the following article, its source, and its intended audience:

(Poletti July 12, 2016).

... "They haven't really evolved to what typical public companies look like at this size and complexity," [the CEO of JPMorgan Chase] said of Tesla. "When you have this kind of ambition, they have to build up credibility with the investor community" ...

... Yet the company and its CEO act as if they are made of Teflon, and don't need to have the types of checks and balances that corporations use to avoid disaster.

"There is a sense that there is a lot on their plate, and this is when you need the right kind of corporate governance structure in place," Diamond [sic] said.

What is clearly at issue concerns the way that corporations are *governed* not only by the boards of directors, but also in every broad sense, including social and regulatory pressures of all kinds. As the discussion continues, the interpretations will be economic *nature. But, economics is not always about money—its nature concerns a logic, a calculus of a kind, concerning how "value" is exchanged in all forms, generally among willing participants.* For example, the politics of swapping favors among influential people is just as economic in *nature* as swapping stocks and bonds. Interested readers may want to investigate a relatively new field called behavioral economics.

Economic Interpretations of Corporate Governance

A significant amount of economics and finance research has investigated the impact of corporate governance on capital investment decisions, though it is difficult to synthesize too many of the specific findings into one consistent policy for all—one theory, if you will. Much study has been idiosyncratic to the specific research scenarios.

Just for the moment, the issue is the distortion of economically rational capital investment decisions made by the board of directors (BODs) *as a group*. In other words, the BOD itself is what researchers call a *unit of analysis*: here, as if it were a single-mined entity like one individual person. One might think of the issue being the *group dynamics* of this one particular kind of group behavior, except the concern is strictly about financial decisions. *A later discussion will address behavioral biases in individuals, that is, the respective executive members.*

Research suggests that any information asymmetries that might exist between corporate managers and external investors are no longer enough to justify using financial logic as the basis of selecting members of a corporate portfolio of companies to own and operate. Again, the modern view says a corporate portfolio should represent a wealth-maximizing diversifity of highly related (if not *synergistic*) competencies and capabilities, which takes expertise and insight, as well as complete information. The issue now is a bit more subtle, more pragmatic, and less abstract. For one thing, the level of analysis shifts from corporations, and their overall levels of performance as the units of analysis of concern, to BODs and their decisions.

Distortions to decisions and decision-making processes used by BODs are caused by the asymmetry of information between managers and shareholders and by manager–shareholder conflicts.

Each of these suggests *agency* problems, which refers to an extensively studied rubric called the *principal–agent theory*. This is first and foremost a branch of economics that studies economically irrationalities caused by imperfections in the principal–agent relationship, that is, an owner–employee relationship, or a boss–subordinate relationship, or an original equipment manufacturer–subcontractor relationship, or many other ways of expressing it, including a shareholder–executive relationship. In short, intentionally or unintentionally and *hidden agendas* aside for the moment, people do not always do what their bosses expect them to do. *Everybody has a boss* even throughout the structure of corporate governance, and there are *economic losses* or costs to the imperfections found not only in relatively informal professional relationships, but also in formal contracts and covenants.

Sometimes (and not always correctly), these imperfections are called "moral hazard" as economic categories go, but this is a poor term, in that no intentional moral lapses are necessarily implied.

Related research similarly suggests that there are three main sets of reasons that explain why investment reasons can be made incorrectly by BODs (Adjaoud, Charfi, and Chourou 2011). First and again, there is what economists call *asymmetric information* that exists between corporate managers and external investors. The information known to each side is not the same as the other side in either quantity or quality, and a common (but very arguable) assumption is that managers have access to more and more complete information *that is relevant to the decision at issue.*

Information asymmetry increases the costs of capital and can cause managers to reject some otherwise worthwhile project opportunities.

The second reason continues the logic previously noted. Again, asymmetric information creates the likelihood of *agency problems*. For example, the managerial incentive to enhance professional careers is not always aligned with the best interest of investors, a kind of moral hazard. This can lead to *empire building* or at least going to lengths to reinforce one's job security, the manipulation of compensation opportunities, and just plain shirking of erstwhile responsibilities.

The many imaginable possibilities of "agency" can lead to either overinvesting or underinvesting, relative to pure economic rationality.

However, a more forgiving view (strictly of the author's) might assert that such managerial indiscretions may actually reflect *economically* rational reactions to the misaligned incentives found in their business relationships. In other words, any economic *immorality* resides structurally in the hazards themselves and is institutional, not in managers' reactions *per se*. On a case-by-case basis, anyway, it serves best to not accuse anyone of anything wrong until incentives are examined. The financial economics researchers being referenced never made any such accusations, but it is worth saying.

Third and aside agency problems, it must be admitted that simple managerial overconfidence may overvalue projects and lead to some of the same bad decisions anyway. A mistake in judgment carries no *moral* insinuation; one way or the other; it is a matter of competence.

Managers can be fired for making mistakes, but not personally sued unless a crime has been committed. This is the essence of separating ownership from management in capitalist philosophy.

More precisely, when one side has quantitatively and qualitatively different information than the other side, this raises the *information risk* to investors and compels from them the demand (as in *supply and demand*) for higher-risk premiums. Consequently, corporate managers underinvest, or in other words, do not approve projects that otherwise might be. Under the conditions noted,

> *external financiers will require a premium creating higher costs of external finance. If this premium is too high, firms should [be expected to] turn down some positive NPV projects rather than raise equity capital ... uninformed* external suppliers of funds interpret equity

issues as bad news (a signal that equity is overvalued) compared to debt issues and demand a large premium (Adjaoud, Charfi, and Chourou 2011, p. 39)

In other words, the relatively uncertain or incomplete nature of shareholder information compels them to command capital investment price premiums (i.e., a higher cost of their capital) above the *correct* rate that would be required under conditions of more *perfect* information available to both sides.

In such instances, project planners' assigned hurdle rates, the cutoffs for go or no-go project decisions become a bit too high and worthwhile project opportunities are foregone. It creates a conservative bias, as opposed to an optimistic one.

Think of the hurdle rate as the acceptable minimum return on an investment, such as a capital project on the whole, that must be demonstrated in the planning process in order for the project to get approved, funded, and started. *Naturally, the hurdle rate itself will vary in accordance with the source and nature of the investment capital.* In contrast to using external capital markets like Wall Street, using internal sources (e.g., retained earnings) suggests lower hurdle expectations, which alludes to one reason some companies get accused of *sitting on piles of cash.* Not only is that view cynical, it is economically irrational. Still, acknowledging that it is not wrong to hold profits in retained earnings (on the liabilities side of a balance sheet, as well as a relatively liquid asset on that side) for a later time when making capital investments is more opportune, it is nevertheless true that imperfections in decision-making regularly occur.

According to what is called the pecking order theory:

... companies prefer using securities that are less sensitive to managers' private information. This infers that managers prefer to finance their new projects with internally generated funds. When externally generated funds are required, firms issue debt followed by various kinds of hybrid debt such as convertible bonds and finally issue equity (Adjaoud, Charfi, and Chourou 2011, p. 39).

The pecking order in the presence of information asymmetry, then, is from internal sources of funding, and then external forms of hybrid debt, and then equity.

Unfortunately, the complexities, complications, and uniqueness of the Tesla situation during the time it issued the specific convertible bonds that became rated *junk* due to cash flow problems alone by the end of 2018 make it difficult to interpret as any version of a pecking order problem. For one thing, while there was media criticism about doing that as opposed to issuing more stock from the beginning, there were certainly no retained earnings (or recent profits or cash) in the sequence to peck from in the first place. The logic in that criticism concerns the matter of possible default that was there from the start. Still, the pecking order problem is interesting.

Again as to one manifestation of moral hazard: "Managers have the incentive to build empires and entrench themselves, or conversely to work less, imitate the decisions of other managers, and take unjustifiable risks" (Adjaoud, Charfi and Chourou 2011, p. 40).

Here, it is fair to infer that *managers* means cadres of less conspicuous and powerful people than Elon Musk was, ostensibly acting alone—middle-level project sponsors and the like who should be involved in the respective decisions. It is edifying to consider differences in leadership styles, which will be left to the reader.

Next, "managers derive private benefits when investing a firm's free cash flow in unprofitable (i.e., negative NPV) projects rather than paying dividends to shareholders."

This may sound shocking because it suggests that managers prefer to invest in failures rather than pay the moneys as dividends; but, this is not what is being suggested. Irrespective of conscious intent, this describes a *moral hazard* that can exist in an *institutional structure*, in that inferior decisions can be made due to the way a corporation is governed by the BOD. Remember that the unit of analysis in this research is the BOD, as a decision-making entity, subject to group behavior phenomena partly due to its composition and structure.

Continuing, "however, insider ownership has the opposite effect. When private benefits are small, an increase in insider ownership attenuates overinvestment but exacerbates underinvestment" (Adjaoud, Charfi, and Chourou 2011, p. 41).

This does add an additional wrinkle, but it is important not to interpret *an increase in insider ownership* as a temporal sequence too literally. It contrasts insider ownership to external ownership, it does not necessarily describe the effect of actually adding greater insider-owner representation to a given BOD. Even if it did, it would be a mistake to assume the opposite causation, that is, of the effect of going public—as the general rule, from less-to-more external and independent representation by owners. Also, it does not necessarily contrast private versus public firms.

On a statistical (research) basis alone, in the relative presence of greater insider ownership compared to external ownership, where the rewards to the members are small as opposed to large, BOD decisions tend to be risk-averse, with both the positive and negative consequences that logically follow.

This does make intuitive sense. People are more careful with their own money than with *house money* in a gaming situation or if you will, *other peoples' money* more politically.

That said, it cannot be suggested that decisions of the Tesla BOD were ever risk-averse on the whole at any time; also, the term *small rewards* does not apply regardless of what *small* could possibly mean. Whether or not the Tesla BOD could have benefited from greater or lesser internal-owner representation is a matter of speculation, especially because Musk was the major stockholder, CEO, and COB. It is probably better to worry about the multiple-role playing by the major investor than this heuristic research finding—in this particular instance. In other words, worrying about the composition of the Tesla board other than Musk, on the basis of this matter of governance as did the media on occasion, could be futile.

Still and more generally, careerism compels managers to

> prefer short-term, lower-valued projects than long-term, higher valued projects ... Managers tend to invest in relatively safe projects for reputational concerns. Further, ... if bad performance is attributed to a common negative shock ... they may prefer to follow the investment decisions of others, leading to suboptimal risk taking (Adjaoud, Charfi and Chourou 2011, p. 41).

The herding idea is interesting, as one issue that was voiced in the media concerned the independence of the Tesla Members of the Board's.

By analogy, herding within a BOD may be likened to a *groupthink* phenomenon in organizational behavior. Groupthink goes beyond cronyism; it is a common effect in any group of people, whether or not they are even peers. *Personalities aside, groups acting as groups tend to make risk-averse decisions.* But, risk-averse does not translate to *best,* because, in the Tesla case, one cannot really hold *personalities aside.*

Even in a BOD of peers, sometimes, it is better to have a strong, even authoritarian leader rather than a relatively communal democracy. Musk was strong and authoritarian, though it is arguable as to whether his decisions were best. The Tesla BOD was not risk-averse at all; the simple observation is that Musk had a profound effect on it. Past that, as MOBs tend to know of each other at least by reputation, that career concern seems valid. Then, the *diversification of employment risk* is no doubt the economist's way of expressing decision-making behaviors that covers one's, let us say, avenues of escape. Altogether, so far the picture is one of a board that must have been—or would have been—more risk-averse than Musk.

Given the preceding quote that leaves to be addressed the time horizons of decisions, which brings the issue back to short-term profit versus the establishment of structural profitability not only for the industry, but more acutely for Tesla and its own reputation with investors.

In its young history, it is again interesting that not only did the Tesla founders not get rich quick(ly) and move on to other adventures, they stuck around and got extraordinarily rich in paper assets, that is, stock. They did this not only by making accounting decisions to plow would-be profits back into internal growth, but also by making strategic decisions that eschewed settling for limited opportunities in small markets, and rather, attacking the mass-market challenge.

They, at least, cannot be accused of short-termism, but pressures coming from Wall Street certainly impacted the BOD into taking a more sensitive stance about near-term investment rewards, as would be expected, right at a time of production crises and cash flow emergencies. Note carefully though, that *near-term investment rewards* is not the same thing as *short-term investment risk.* While it must be true that some of the Wall Street pressure came from relative latecomers with short-term investment concerns—*traders* if you will—it was just as certain that much of the pressure was coming from people who had invested years earlier. Then, wisely or not, they had long-term hopes not only for electric vehicles (EVs), but many also had hopes or the fate of the planet. In any case, collectively, they were not only getting impatient about positive returns, but also worried about outright solvency and collapse. To say that the board did "prefer short-term, lower-valued projects [to] long-term, higher valued projects" would miss the point that the costs of capital were simply coming due.

Four Main Sources of Concern

The literature describes four sets of concerns, addressing at once the BODs, ownership structure, managerial compensation, and leverage:
   BODs:

> The *governance role played by the BOD in reducing investment distortions is limited. First, the CEO may control the information received by the board, which affects the board's judgment. Second, ... career concerns tempt the board to overinvest during economic upturns and to underinvest during economic downturns* (Adjaoud, Charfi and Chourou 2011, p. 47).

These findings, of course, are all unfortunate. The sum of it might be to say that boards *do no harm*, and that would be a bit optimistic.

As it concerns Tesla, it suggests that the impact of information distortion may have even been exaggerated by Musk's dual role of CEO and COB, and that leaves aside issues of personality and ownership. As to the career concerns of other MOBs, there were no notable statements in the media that related to economic conditions; but, for that matter, there were no reports of any major project disapprovals at all. Anyway, at this point, it bears noting that *independence* is sometimes a matter of degree and kind; here, the main issue is stock ownership. On the other hand, many MOBs are well-enough compensated for their services to include that as a career concern in the same vein as equity ownership. Nothing is being accused, though—one would have to have access to minutes of meetings to truly give a good assessment. Media items hardly contain that level of fidelity, which is a good example of *information asymmetry* with some irony in itself.

Ownership structure:

[E]nhanced monitoring by large shareholders decreases the overinvestment of free cash flows … however, … concentrated share ownership is unrelated to the magnitude of the free cash flow, suggesting that large shareholders are not particularly effective in solving the free cash flow problem (Adjaoud, Charfi and Chourou 2011, p. 48).

The *free cash flow problem*, of course, starts with making any of it at all—think of free cash flow as the absolute returns to a project, the margin of main interest.

While Tesla was widely held by many *retail investors*, at the same time, much of its market cap was held by just a few prominent players who became quite vocal, even calling for Musk's replacement. Of course, the simplicity of the finding is confounded once more, by Musk being all of CEO, COB, and the major stockholder by far. Not surprisingly, the BOD stuck with Musk:

(Barrabi May 1, 2018).

"Although … one person, could provide an effective leadership for Tesla at the early stage, now in this much more highly competitive and rapidly changing technology industry, it is more and more difficult to oversee Tesla's business" [a spokesperson for stockholders] wrote …

Tesla's board of directors … supported Musk "… the Company's success to date would not have been possible if the Board was led by another director … In light of the significant future opportunities for growth and the careful execution needed in order for the Company to achieve it, the Board believes that the Company is still best served by Mr. Musk continuing to serve as Chairman."

Then, while it might be inferred from the research that these voices initially had a good effect on *making* investment decisions, their subsequent impact on cash flow problems *that the decisions created* was muted. Altogether, that would be a negative effect.

The research also suggests that *corporations that are not well-governed tend to make acquisitions as opposed to similar internal investments in capital and R&D that would likely be more profitable* (Adjaoud, Charfi and Chourou 2011, p. 49). This is difficult to assess at Tesla, though, because strategic management research also shows that acquisitions get faster results than internal development. As such, not only do the time value of money calculations affect any comparison, but even more so, strategic timing and concerns such as first-mover advantage. To forgo the latter would be an opportunity cost of the same capital. Recall that Tesla's acquisition of SolarCity was controversial; but, because Elon Musk was its principal owner too, the instance would be considered anomalous from the theoretical standpoint. It was very meaningful, but it was so meaningful it should stand as its own case study. Otherwise, Tesla made a few acquisitions, but it was hardly a spree.

Managerial compensation:

> *If the owners know the managers' employment opportunities, invest-*
> *ment alternatives, and risk preferences ... a managerial compensation*
> *contract may be structured to act in the shareholders' best interests ...*
> *On the other hand, the ... contract depends on the characteristics of*
> *the firm's investment opportunities as well as ... managerial prefer-*
> *ences for capital* (Adjaoud, Charfi and Chourou 2011, p. 46).

This issue should not even be addressed here, once again, because of the *information asymmetries* that one must assume existed between the Tesla BOD, the media, and the author—the latter being particularly in the dark. In any event, it is interesting that the following article appeared only a few months before Musk's ouster attempt happened in the media:

(No author January 22, 2018).

... Tesla announced Tuesday that it would *pay Musk nothing* for the next 10 years — no salary, bonus or stock — unless the electric car company nearly doubles in value ...

... the new pay plan encourages Musk to focus on increasing sales, profits and the Tesla stock price without holding him accountable to meeting production quotas. It also untethers him from ... the only outstanding hurdle from the 2012 agreement ... [to] maintain a gross margin of at least 30 percent for four consecutive quarters. The last time Tesla's gross margin was that high was the first quarter of 2012.

At the face value, that excerpt is fairly plain, but the full article is difficult to decipher. Musk's contract held him to meeting 10 operational goals, which should relate to financial goals like revenues from sales and gross margin, and in turn market cap and stock options, but production quotas were not among them. It is unclear how all this can happen without the latter. As the production of the 300,000th vehicle was a goal, however, it might be that the board felt that meeting quotas just for the sake of meeting quotas was not really *the issue*. In other words, it was not really a production scheduling problem in the grandest strategic sense. This certainly would forgive some of the promises quoted often in the media—forgiven by the BOD, that is.

Leverage: "Overinvestment can be mitigated by issuing debt because managers will be forced to use free cash flow to pay the debt service instead of investing in wasteful projects ... However, excess debt may also lead to underinvestment decisions" (Adjaoud, Charfi, and Chourou 2011, p. 44). The general impression on Wall Street increasingly became the suspicion of unbridled overinvestment, at least where the timing of cash flow was concerned. Several months after the previous article appeared:

(Higgins March 15, 2018).

... Tesla must boost production of the Model 3 or possibly face severe financial consequences ... Meeting the goal of 5,000 Model 3s a week by the end of June is critical to generating enough cash to sustain operations without having to raise more capital ...

... Tesla is no longer a startup ... Mr. Musk has eschewed operating profit and racked up debt ... He had earlier pledged to deliver 500,000 vehicles this year, about five times last year's total ...

"Some big investors are losing patience," said [an analyst] ... "They are less excited about it than they were a year ago."

In sum, it is impossible to say with confidence what might have been different in the Tesla story, had Elon Musk not been all of largest investor, CEO, and COB. The literature cited here generally assumes a clear and more classic division of labor among executive roles. This is wise from the research standpoint because *role ambiguity confounds principal–agent problems.* This does not even include roles Musk adopted on an *ad hoc* basis, such as the *de facto* COO *du jour.* Aside some members of the board, who did become vocal and influential, at the face value, it could be said that Musk was something of a one-man governance structure. Then, add to this dry economics the impact of personality, charisma, vision, and the like. In retrospect *vis-a-vis* the aforementioned articles, consider the prescience of the following, which appeared two years earlier:

(Tobak August 04, 2016).

... Tesla is no longer a startup, which begs the question: Are Musk's skills suitable to scaling and running a mainstream car company? Musk is a creator. An inventor. An innovator. As long as Tesla was in startup mode – building limited production high-priced vehicles – he managed to perform. But in terms of operations and execution on everything from product pricing and production to cash flow and profits, his track record has been abysmal.

... scaling that Tesla into a mainstream electric car company capable of flawless execution ... presents an entirely different set of problems ... And to me, it looks like it is simply not in his DNA.

It is probably best to leave genetic predispositions an open question in an economic analysis, so this section will end here.

Managerial Biases in Investment Decisions

The preceding section suggests that there is nothing purely scientific when groups make *rational* economic decisions; extending that, the focus shifts more to the *individual* human psychology of executive decision making. The following review is based on research on *discounting*, in particular, but also has general implications for managing capital projects.

Defaulting to Judgment

Applying judgment is an important and necessary role of managers. Strategic decisions are no exception and on balance using judgment is probably a good thing, especially considering the importance of unique-ness in the pursuit of any true competitive advantage. As well, the *myth* that true innovation is a matter of pure instinct and defies rationalization and corporatization goes too far, but it does contain a grain of empiri-cal truth. The evidence about Musk makes plain that many people and institutions trusted his judgment to the tune of billions of dollars of invested capital, enough to surpass General Motors, and so on. That much cannot be denied.

Smallish projects can be adjudicated well with good judgment, and sensi-tivity analysis can be used one project at a time.

This approach may be justified if the project is sufficiently small in monetary terms or if decision are made by vote of a capital budgeting committee, executive committee, or board of directors … The main use of the judgement approach is to supplement and support other more scientific and prudent techniques (Arnold and Nixon 2011, p. 219).

The same research found, though, that people are prone to collect informa-tion and substitute judgment instead. The implication is that the informa-tion collection phase may have been a waste of time, or close.

Sense-Making

More clinically, these are called representativeness and availability biases. *"Individuals evaluate the probability of an event depending on similarities of that event with well-known classes, disregarding evidence about the underlying probabilities. Consequently, they usually find patterns in random data"* (Biondi and Marzo 2011, p. 423). When evaluating a project, a decision maker may say "I've seen this before," when in reality, the image would correctly be understood to be an illusion. It is perhaps the case that EV naysayers suffered this bias, that is, that Tesla was a *car company* doomed to fail.

"People are also affected by the so-called 'law of small numbers,' which is the tendency to believe that even small-sized samples should reflect the properties of the parent population" (Biondi and Marzo 2011, p. 423).

In logic, this very common error is called the *inductive fallacy*, that is, drawing generalizations from sample sizes too small to be useful in such a way. This is the same error that is assiduously avoided when researchers use large sample sizes. Not so popularly known is that a *very* large sample size, say, several hundred or thousand, is only needed in order to assure that the sample size is representative of the population on the whole. If representativeness of a smaller sample can be assured, a small sample can be properly be used. This is why sample sizes of 25 or 30 are acceptable if sampling *techniques* are proper in the first place.

As it concerns projects, representativeness may not sound hard to assure, but remember that the main issue is innovation, which means some degree of uniqueness by definition.

Aside that, it is problematic to assume that experience with anything less than a few dozen projects that share important similarities to a given project proposal is a good enough basis to depend on experience alone. At Tesla, anyway, there was no such database of representative real-world experience for decision makers to refer to. One might be able to count at most a dozen global EV attempts and then, apply them only very carefully, as they were all different business propositions. This error is no less dangerous than *sampling on the dependent variable*, which is to only consider *positives* and overlook the non-events. The point concerning this bias is to point to the opposite as it concerns Tesla. While it might sound risky

COMMUNICATION AND STAKEHOLDER MANAGEMENT   83

to some, starting over with clean-sheet designs and a different business model worked for Tesla at least in the early going, much to the delight of investors in those early times.

Per the availability bias,

> The easier is the recollection of an event, the higher will be the probability assigned to its occurrence ... people *make estimates starting from an initial value (anchoring) and then adjusting it in order to find out the final answer over a series of trial and errors ... Such* a bias can affect estimations of cash flow representations (Biondi and Marzo 2011, p. 423).

Anchoring effects are found in various types of decision scenarios, but here is mention of cash flow specifically. Extending the given hypothetical, the decision maker may base judgments about a project proposal's estimated cash flow using his or her experience with previous projects, anchoring financial expectations to, say, the average of that.

Just as one of countless possibilities, an odd one is this. An experienced industry executive might think but not say, "Our overly ambitious project sponsors 'always' make projections that turn out to be optimistic by about 25 percent. I should fudge this project proposal accordingly." Again, this is not to suggest whether or not this is a good idea; just that, it may not accord with proposal data that was honestly and carefully developed.

Next, the *prospect theory* also takes into account the framing effect and anchoring.

> *[E]very prospect's value is a function of a reference point, usually the status quo or an aspiration level ... an individual frames the value function in terms of gains or losses with respect to his or her own reference point* (Biondi and Marzo 2011, p. 424).

Let us not try to get into Elon Musk's mind on all of this, but it is true that prior to joining Tesla, he had experienced great bounty resulting from his own decisions, which could provide a powerful anchor indeed.

The next part is particularly interesting, in that not only is it a behavioral effect *apart* from economic rationality, it is itself *irrational.*

"[N]ot only do individuals fail to show a unique and positive relationship in the risk-return relationship (subsumed by compound discounting), but they also tend to change the direction of this relationship depending on the way they frame decisions" (Biondi and Marzo 2011, p. 424). This is a bit stunning for any decision maker who is familiar with the basics of finance. *Everybody knows* that there is a positive relationship between risk and return, but this slice of research shows that the understanding can be reversed due to a framing effect! To reverse the risk-return axiom is to assume that high risks are associated with a lower return (or vice versa).

This would hardly apply to the typical Tesla investor, but it is interesting. Just to speculate, perhaps, an individual may misunderstand probability math, and subjectively inject an additional amount of pessimism based on previous EV failures, irrationally lowering the true expected value of the investment. To be careful though, it would be graceful to posit that the framing effect would have to be profoundly different, as no trained businessperson imagines such a relationship.

On a related note, it is common to assume that prices will always rise, and that there will always be some degree of inflation. We frame the future this way as a matter of course, so some manner of discounting happens instinctively—or at least reflexively after a little bit of professional conditioning. But, in the modern era, and in the kind of decisions mostly assumed in these discussions, these assumptions bear constant re-visiting.

For example, prices do not always go up because, as examples: economies of scale (in right-sized facilities) and scope (including platform designs) should achieve lower unit costs and unit prices; commodity prices are volatile; oil and lithium and all else are rarely in lockstep; advancements in things like robotics and artificial intelligence (AI) will greatly improve efficiencies and thereby real facility capacities beyond crude measures like footprint; industrial and personal productivity generally rises, as well as inflation although they have opposite effects on prices, and so forth. In fact, this is exactly the strategic utility of using learning curves in the first place. These effects are deflationary, just more local to an industry, a market, or situationally to a specific project.

Even when merely *adjusting for inflation*, this is to net the assumed inflation effect on everything, equally, netting that assumption against the worse assumption—that nothing, at all, will change. The framing effect of mindlessly assuming inflation can backfire on a decision, and partly explains the utility of approaches like risk-neutral pricing in real options (Volume II, this series). Anyway, be assured that there is a positive relationship between risk and return in the vast majority of cases, and this axiom is worth counting on unless contradictory information is very unusual and compelling.

Perceptions About Time

It makes sense that the effects of the impact of the time value of money (and discounted cash flow (DCF) methods) would be biased by one's experience with time itself. At issue is bias concerning *perceptions* of discount rates.

First, the "common difference" effect says that the longer the project planning horizon, the lower the discount rate all else held equal.

Second and in what is called the "absolute magnitude" effect, large amounts of invested capital are less discounted than small ones, on a proportional basis.

Third, there is what is called "delay-speedup asymmetry." Another framing effect, it implies an "asymmetric preference between speeding up a loss and delaying a gain. *A greater amount is then required to compensate for delaying an incoming reward ... than for anticipating (speeding up) a loss by the same interval"* (Biondi and Marzo 2011, pp. 424–425). The asymmetry becomes somewhat alarming when one realizes that the former effect is about two to four times greater than the latter effect. Combining the two, the effect on the discount rate varies not only with the size of the expected payoff, but also whether it is positive or negative. The magnitude of the asymmetry should give a planner pause. Past that, the psychology is complex.

As it concerns Tesla, it seems quite possible that decisions were intertemporally biased because (a) time delays were commonplace and *became* more-or-less *priced into* investor expectations of production forecasts (one might even say *with a wink and a nod* from Wall Street that became the norm); (b) the amounts of capital involved were very substantial; and (c) when push came to shove, actual, experienced delays exceeded anyone's hopes and aspirations, polarizing stakeholder camps severely. More cautiously, all that will be asserted is that discount rates on things like bonds may have been *irrationally* determined from the outset and made worse as time went on, as it is a fact that a bad crisis resulted that threatened the company in its entirety. Still, these effects are very complex in combination.

Expectations About Cash Flows

The following biases are not difficult to understand and are probably everyday experiences in human affairs. There are biases called plainly enough, optimism and overconfidence.

> "If the *description of the company is very favorable, a very high profit will appear representative of that description; if the description is mediocre, a mediocre performance will appear most representative"*… *the human mind appears to work as a pattern-seeking device. This leads decision-makers to give rational meaning to events that can be random* (Biondi and Marzo 2011, p. 427).

This is not quite the same thing as presented earlier; it involves external estimations of cash flow, not so much internal estimations.

A related research expression is the *false-positive* notion, except here, it is assumed to be caused by biased perceptions alone. *False positives do not always happen in conditions of true randomness, but also in patterns of data that do not confidently warrant conclusions about apparent positive evidence. Confidence* is a matter of deeper statistical analysis of things that appear at face value.

As it concerns Tesla, media presentations changed greatly over a short period, carefully granting the benefit of the doubt for years, to becoming very worried about bond covenants specifically. Mentions about cash flow and, specifically, corporate-level free cash flow came up often, coupled with mentions about only ever declaring a quarterly profit twice, and more specious concerns about in effect, structural profitability. But, it is hard to accuse that bias as being psychologically dysfunctional, not to mention economically irrational. The history of similar experiences would certainly support it.

Sunk Costs Versus Committed Investments

This all-too-common form of economic irrationality is one that a person learns about in any beginning economics curriculum. Here, though, it becomes vital to maintain the distinction between an expense and an investment.

In the author's experience, sunk costs are generally thought of (implicitly or explicitly) as *expenses* that have already been incurred, where the idea is that the past is the past and nothing can be done about it anymore. Projects funded in operating budgets have been implicitly characterized that way. Situations vary, but cannot be stylized here; the point is that, when it comes to investments, not all money spent in the past is in the economic meaning, money gone (Biondi and Marzo 2011).

This is not a subtle distinction, but the research largely ignores it. Operationally speaking, including projects funded in the operating budget, money spent is money gone, though the expense *should have been "worth it." This stands in contrast with an investment funded in a capital budget. There, a delay is fully expected from the very beginning, and the time horizon can be many years, sometimes as with science and technology, decades.*

However, this is not the place to argue, say, the pros and cons of public subsidization of science, versus venture capital, versus public ownership, and so forth. It will just be asserted that these institutions exist to sort out this very problem. The general idea is still valid and about psychology, not economics. Still, note the ambiguous terms: "[People] are more likely to continue a bad project if they have already made a prior *investment* ... the scale is unrelated to the perception of failure." It seems that "the past is relevant because it contains information which changes the image of the future; the probabilities which govern future actions are modified by observations on the past" (Biondi and Marzo 2011, p. 429).

Either way, it would be natural for the decision makers at Tesla to be victimized by this bias. Pressure was particularly acute during the time when Tesla experienced so much agony, making the transition from (likely profitable) niche markets, to (dubiously profitable) mass markets. The longstanding commitment was to save the planet, but simple survival came into doubt. The media did suggest an epiphany on all sides of the issue. The real issue, though, is having the foresight and wisdom to draw the distinction between entrepreneurial (Schumpeterian) irrationality and in reality, *throwing good money after bad.*

Escalating Commitment to a Failing Course of Action

These same words are the actual title of a known psychological phenomenon and strain of research. This effect can be understood as a variation of the sunk cost effect, with the additional assumption that *evidence of eventual failure seems rather plain in the present,* and available to all. Not only do sunk costs become chased, the intensity of a *foolish* chase gets worse and worse, and in some cases, downright crazy. *Even when evidence of impending failure becomes apparent, escalation of the commitment rises in ways that can be truly irrational.*

> [C]ontinued inve*stment in a* project when expected future results are negative and suggest abandoning it ... is no*w recognized as a major pitfall in the control of an investment project* ... Individual commitment is usually rewarded ... pursuing a failing course of action can then result from the inability of decision makers to free themselves from the social norms (Biondi and Marzo 2011, p. 430).

On *social norms,* however, it may also be noted that the *rationality* of career politics (as opposed to classic economic rationality) is a common phenomenon because tenacity is considered a virtue. Even in economics, such *transactions* are meaningful and studied as principal–agent problems. Finally,

> *Every business activity constitutes a special relational economic context. Its decision makers receive information through numerous channels that treat and reduce that information by various ways and under special conditions ... Because this process is laden with ignorance, hazard, and dynamics, the information is typically blurred or filtered information, meaning that some aspects of the information may be obscured or lost* (Biondi and Marzo 2011, p. 436).

Against that admonition, of course, is the commonsense suggestion that the fidelity of planning data, namely, the ultimate outcomes of future uncertainties on final cash flows, is not as important as the overall wisdom needed to make good basic strategic decisions.

The Bottom Line: So to Speak

From the behavioral (and research) point of view, the preceding discussion focused on main effects. There are secondary or side-effects, too. On the whole, the news is good, but not without a few qualifications. Some terms that may be unfamiliar to the reader are explained at length later, mostly in Volume II of this series.

> In the [project] developmental stage, most firms agree that cash flows are the appropriate cost-benefit data ... including the consideration of opportunity costs ... In the selection stage, the use of DCF analysis as the primary selection tool has steadily increased while the use of the payback period in the main analysis has steadily declined. The use of the WACC has also increased ... Managers recognize risk differences in projects and adjust the hurdle rate, albeit on an ad hoc *basis* (Mukherjee and Al Rahahleh 2011, pp. 166–167).

On the other hand, the same body of research says that compared to their respective pros and cons in different real scenarios, the internal rate of return (IRR) is often incorrectly preferred to the net present value (NPV), the use of payback may be used too often and be given too high a priority, and capital rationing is sometimes overdone. More specifically:

> [First,] Firms might prefer IRR because of its comparability with returns from returns of other investment opportunities ... [Second,] All firms require project sponsors to compute both NPV and IRR ... emphasis on IRR might lead to incorrect decisions... [Third] When a conflict occurs ... most firms rank the project by their IRRs but select the bundle that maximizes a firm's overall NPV (Mukherjee and Al Rahahleh 2011, pp. 166–167).

Of course, imperfections of method matter most if they turn good decisions into bad ones, that is, whether they reject viable project proposals or accept bad ones. Managers who use these methods should understand their advantages and disadvantages with respect to their (a) industries, (b) corporate strategies, and (c) specific project decisions.

Conclusion

This chapter takes mostly the executive view of managing capital projects, here attending to two knowledge areas in the Project Management Institute paradigm—project communication management and project stakeholder management. As the deployment of investor capital is the acute underlying issue, fiduciary responsibilities there immediately turn into a concern for corporate governance, specifically. Fortunately, rigorous economic and finance research has been performed in the issues, which was reviewed and interpreted *vis-à-vis* the Tesla experience. In this way, the chapter anticipates much more economic rigor concerning capital project budgeting that dominates Volume II in this series.

Discussion Questions

How can *bureaucratic* processes, methods, and structures be used constructively in the management of innovation?

Considering the pros and cons of *going public*, what is the right time for an IPO, considering managing fiduciary responsibilities to external stakeholders?

What is corporate governance? How is today's environment different from the past, and what does research suggest will be trendy in the future?

What is *moral hazard*, how is it that it occurs, and how do similar *agency* problems impact capital project decisions?

Discuss how biases in investment decision processes distort the *rational* cost of capital and in turn, capital project discount or hurdle rates.

CHAPTER 5

Principles of Project Management

Introduction

One of the unsung advantages of any standard technology is how much innovation it stimulates, that is, innovation that complies with the standard. As discussions about dominant designs pointed out, once one appears, innovation that does not comply with the standard tends to drop precipitously. Not until a radically different idea comes along, does the standard become replaced or, at least, radically revised. This is true about just about any kind of standard.

The closest thing to a standard approach to project management is that of the Project Management Institute (PMI) in the United States. It publishes and periodically revises *A Guide to the Project Management Body of Knowledge*, or PMBOK, which itself is an ANSI Standard. The PMI also provides an accreditation to university programs, and most, if not all, project management textbooks adopt it as a main reference in any case. The Project Management Professional (PMP) certification is generally recognized as the most prestigious of its kind, and many contracts require it of project team leaders. The PMI also awards a PMP and other competency-specific certifications and publishes other standards that are directly related to this book: risk management, portfolio management, schedule, cost, and others. In short, PMI is considered best practice globally.

The PMI paradigm is universal and accommodates virtually any project, including the kind of capital projects considered in this book. However, neither the PMI library nor the general collection of university texts published by others nor the popular press does much to provide detailed guidance about capital project finance. It was this observation that largely motivated the development of this series. To help complete the picture, this chapter outlines the PMI paradigm with capital projects in mind.

After Studying this Chapter, the Reader will be Able to

Explain how a project management approach is well-suited to managing capital projects individually and in portfolios.

Describe various ways a firm can be organized for project management from the top of the organization chart.

Give examples of why managing trade-offs is at the heart of project management as an organization wide capability.

Critique the relative importance of the knowledge areas under different management scenarios.

Define: project, scope, charter, statement of work, constraint, and deliverable.

Project Management as an Organizing Principle

Many corporations are organized by division, product line, or industry served, and each of these is hypothetically a representative of a different asset class (see Volume II) by which to consider systematic project risks in discount rates and hurdle rates. In this section, the general assumption is that this has already been accomplished if appropriate. In other words, most concerns from there are intra-divisional. With that assumed, the discussion will proceed using a basic rubric for organizing projects that first poses two extreme cases, and then something in the middle. The two extreme cases are the pure project organization and the classic functional organization, and the compromise in the middle is called the matrix organization.

Interested readers should consult the vast literature known as the organizational theory (Daft 2004; Scott 1993). This field is not the same as organizational behavior. The former focuses on organized groups on the whole, while the latter focuses on human behavior in groups. Both fields have been central contributors to management for over a century (Wren 2003).

The Functional Organization

As the industrial revolution progressed throughout the 19th and 20th centuries, technology advanced faster than *management* could adjust. *This happened in several ways, but none was more obvious than about how to organize a scale-based economy, one firm at a time. At that time, the major imperative was to rationalize production or, in other words, make it more efficient.* In plain terms, high-tech business in factories was a mess, and compared to the sole experience of running agrarian-based economies, it was far from obvious what to do about it.

It was found that the most efficient way to organize was along the lines of job function, or job specialization, a kind of division of labor. It soon became more than common, for example, for accountants to work in a single department with other accountants, engineers with engineers, personnel people with other personnel people, and so forth. This was not just common sense at the time. The idea went beyond the obvious instance when people worked near each other and were sequentially dependent, for example, along assembly lines. It was also true when *mutual adjustment* among similarly skilled people enhanced their overall efficacy both as individuals and as work units.

This "economic function" kind of structure also became known more simply as the "functional organization."

This term has nothing to do with *level* of competence *per se*, but rather, refers to the *commonality* of job functions among its members. It applies whenever people are more basically grouped by skill-based similarities than by their differences—for example, the *business guys* versus the *floor guys*. The allusion to somewhat different professional cultures is intentional as well, and it can matter.

In the simplest case, efficiency is a matter of meeting a target level of production while minimizing wasted resources—labor, raw, materials, overhead, time, and everything in between (Fairtlough 1994; Scott 1993).

This is especially seen in mature industries, where cost-based competitive advantage is a common goal, dominant designs exist, regulations abound, configuration management is strict, and "bureaucracy" can choke innovation.

However, where innovation and not efficiency is the imperative itself, things work well (if not best) when people are "taken from" functional units and formed into multi disciplinary teams.

Whether considering a small team working on an *operational* project with a not-to-exceed budget, or a *bet the company* capital project working as a separate business unit with profit objectives, sometimes, being efficient is not as important as being effective at accomplishing an *output*, a result, a strategic objective.

Such a dilemma poses an obvious management challenge. For example, there may be many informal multidivisional teams working all over an organization on an *ad hoc* basis, without a hint about it on the top-level organization chart. If left unmanaged, some unintended effects can be serious enough to wreck an organization over time, so alternatives are needed.

The Pure Project Organization

By nature, it was never possible for some industries or major lines of business to organize by economic function. This has always been particularly true of what are now called *fixed position layout* production schemes, where the final product stays in place. This is a kind of production concept where an entire product must be developed not just *in situ*, but at one exact spot from where it will never be moved.

Examples abound in construction industries. Whole sections such as rook lattices are often partly fabricated elsewhere, and then the sub-assemblies are joined *in situ*. In fact, there are *pre-fabs* and *trailers*, too, that are just trucked to the home site and positioned, though not necessarily forever. Still, it is unusual for a finished house to ever again be moved—or a bridge, or a dam, or a pyramid.

Sometimes, a line of business must have a fixed-position production scheme due to technology alone. Phased or not, then, it is common for each production end-item to be organized as a project all its own, and a whole company can be organized project-by-project even at the top level of an organization chart. This can happen when a final product is intensely customized and very costly, even one-of-a-kind—say, the Hubble Telescope.

When this happens, it can result in what is sometimes referred to as a pure project organization. The geographical imperative for the separation of projects is only meant to be a clear image, however. The same principle can apply if driven by other imperatives, such as the strategic wisdom of keeping each project focused on its own particular market in order to create an atmosphere of customer orientation and response, project-by-project.

Some organizations are organized project-by-project even at the highest level, disregarding the benefits of grouping people by specialization except below that structure.

Such an organizing scheme is inviting to organizations with the kind of capital projects that have been described as *bet the company* endeavors, which in cases like Tesla (e.g., Roadster, Model 3) are no exaggeration at all. Constraints such as stakeholder transparency, *profitability* of specific projects, and even keeping Generally Accepted Accounting Principles (GAAP) quarterly or annual reporting can sometimes leave little other option.

In the middle, so to speak, is the matrix organization. The matrix and ideas like it are plain evidence that large and old organizations are indeed capable of learning from more *entrepreneurial* younglings.

Matrix Organizations

The advantages and disadvantages of the economic function organization and the pure project organization are well studied and understood. The matrix form is a conscious effort to establish a working optimum. Naturally, the textbook matrix is idealized just like the two extremes, and every situation is likely to be unique enough to require some adaptation. In fact, employee training and professionalism are key components, and any organization chart is likely to not fully represent how people get it done. But, the organization chart is still helpful and is the best way to begin an understanding.

It takes a certain ability to think abstractly, but first imagine an org chart that looks like the classic economic function type, and then imagine an *overlay* of a periodically changing pure project type of organization laid perpendicularly to it. The classical, vertical lines of functional authority intersect at right angles with horizontal lines that connect individual workers who are members of project teams, each led by a project manager. Each economic function is the regular administrative home of all the workers sharing the same specialization that circumscribes the departmental function, but individuals are temporarily assigned the responsibility to respond to the project manager for project-related things.

Now, it must be admitted that assigning a temporary responsibility to someone who is not even a member of one's home department invites accountability problems alone. This scheme might sound like the invention of pure chaos, but again, many organizations do this successfully, and there is no shortage of empirical findings that explain its pros and cons.

A well-working matrix organization needs professionalism and some modicum of dedication by all involved. Training can help; depending on "common sense" is risky.

Some kinds of conflicts are almost inevitable—role ambiguity, promotion and advancement, changing job locations for short periods—and some *personal adjustment* is regularly required. Administrative and project managers may experience resource and scheduling conflicts, even among each other. Executives may need to intercede. It is not unfair to say that it is one of those things that works about as well as people want it to. It is not perfect, but in any given organization, it may work much better than either extreme case.

Project Management Overview

The PMI defines a project as *"A temporary endeavor undertaken to create a unique product, service, or result"* (PMI-PMBOK 2017). This definition is not confined to capital projects, operational projects, business projects, or for that matter, any other kind of formally organized endeavor. For that matter, no organization need exists at all, at least not as usually imagined. It can apply to a personal effort to throw an elaborate wedding, or to build an extension on a house needing subcontractors, or a government endeavor to send a person to Mars "by the end of this decade and return him [or her] safely to the earth," and just about everything in between. The principles are much the same across the board.

The nature of new product development in the modern era practically makes project management a necessity (Brentani and Kleinschmidt 2015; Sicotte, Drouin, and Delerue 2014).

Again, it is important to define terms. In the definition of a project, *temporary* is not necessarily the same thing as *short term* and rarely will be in the case of capital projects. All the term really means is that a project is intended to not last forever, like an *operations program*, such as ongoing manufacturing. More to the point, projects have serious deadlines for total project accomplishment and then, formal closeout and shutdown. In the author's view, whereas programs and operations might be said to *fail* if they ever stop, projects fail if they drag on very much past the original deadline. Nevertheless, the kind of capital projects of interest here are generally of strategic importance and sometimes *bet the company*.

The goal of a capital project is to make an economically real return on the investment, called economic value-added (EVA). Free cash flow is not EVA, but it is close. Because of impact of time on the cost of capital alone, deadlines matter!

Next, projects are said to be unique, which usually means that their goals are, to some extent, new. Technical uniqueness is not the only kind needed to define a project, but this is generally true. In the present case, discussions have used dichotomies that describe innovation like incremental versus discontinuous, but by no means should uniqueness necessarily be taken to mean discontinuous, radical, or *breakthrough*. It just means that there is sufficient newness in the overall set of objectives that they require a unique project effort; otherwise, it probably would not happen, or happen *well*, or happen *on time*, or happen at acceptable *cost*.

That said, projects are said to be constrained. *A constraint is "an applicable restriction or limitation, either internal or external to the project that will affect the performance of the project or a process"* (PMI-PMBOK 2017). *The three classic constraints are (technical) scope, schedule, and cost.* Capital projects have clear, formal, and relatively non-negotiable deadlines, budgets, and *deliverables* that can be defined by measurable and contractually enforceable standards. Standards can be formal or *de facto*, such as might be the case by a dominant design. Other kinds of constraints (e.g., resources, time, and quality) have been added to the classic three, but upon inspection, many of them can be seen to be derivative of time, money, and technical scope.

A typical quip of the project manager is something like "you can have it on time, under budget, or done right—pick two." This speaks to the real competency set of the project manager, which is to manage constraint trade-offs.

Not only is it a natural reality that a change in one constraint usually affects either or both of the other constraints, but the planning makes it almost inevitable. For example, technology goals are intentionally set aggressive and challenging enough, to not have much *slack* in them to accommodate any ongoing improvements without a negative effect on schedule and cost.

The same can be said where the main priority is not technical, but a matter of timing, or a matter of available money. In fact, *slack*, first and foremost, is a technical measure of how long a project can be delayed before the deadline is threatened, suggesting at face value that time, not technology, is of the essence. *Discussions in this series note the importance of timing and not speed per se; as well, the importance not only of capital budgeting, but of the cost of capital as the final "hurdle" before EVA and any claim to competitive advantage* (stressed in Volume II). In the abstract, then, no one constraint is any more independent, or important, than another when it comes to capital projects.

The PMI Knowledge Areas and Capital Projects

As in any field of management, effective project management is embedded in a strategic context. For present purposes, it does not matter whether the strategy is corporate or business—multidivisional or single-indus-try—though the main strategic concern for capital projects is corporate, regardless of how many lines of business are involved. This is a hair that no longer needs to be split. As well, many capital projects are such major endeavors that in print, one can seem like a mixture of a strategic plan and a business plan, all in one project proposal, complete with a mission statement and its conceptual derivatives like clear strategic objectives.

By dint of thinking through constraints and their trade-offs, a major capital project planner is almost forced to make clear what the plan will do and by clear exclusion, what opportunities it will forgo down to rel-atively small scheduling and budget details. This is characteristic of any good strategy, information permitting. That said, it is natural to first con-sider project integration as the first knowledge area in the project man-agement (PM) paradigm.

Project Integration

This label is more or less self-explanatory, considering all there is to manage. *This is where managing constraint trade-offs becomes a constant challenge. The trade-offs are not only among the major constraints, but over time.* Consider first, this view of investor concern as a beginning point for strategic planning for say, the upcoming year 2018:

(Sage and Panchadar November 1, 2017).

Tesla Inc. on Wednesday pushed back its target for volume production ... saying it was difficult to predict how long it would take to fix all production bottlenecks.

Tesla ... faces a crucial test in its growth strategy as it ramps up production of the Model 3 ... The company said it now expects to build 5,000 Model 3s per week by late in the first quarter of 2018 ...

Model 3 production delays ... exacerbate the company's cash burn ... The problems could also worry the over 500,000 customers who have put down a refundable deposit on the car.

About six months later, how were things going?

(Higgins and Pulliam June 28, 2018).

... Mr. Musk wanted to reinvent the assembly process ... with the goal of making a total of 500,000 vehicles, including other models, in 2020 ...

His executives pushed back, warning it wasn't feasible because the design of the car wasn't yet locked into place, the robots and tooling needed to be ordered, and time was needed to work out inevitable kinks in the complicated assembly process ...

Mr. Musk concedes he relied too much on automation. "You really want to get the process nailed down and then automate, as opposed to assuming you know what the process will be, then automating that."

A lesson to take from the preceding excerpts is that some better planning may have avoided *production hell* at Tesla. Uncertainties were rife, and many difficulties were difficult to foresee, but accounts like this do suggest that Musk underestimated not only the problems of scaling up to mass-manufacturing, but also the transition from design to manufacturing writ large. Risk management is one of the most important knowledge areas in the PM paradigm, and managing the integration of investment risk and technology risk alone, suggests opportunities forgone at Tesla.

Now, consider *scaling up* as a project unto itself, that is, focused as much on measurable productivity-efficiency goals as production-total goals. Or possibly, one so concerned with production economics that total production goals were clearly secondary until the scaling-up project was practically completed. In fact, total production goals would become an ongoing operations program immediately thereafter, and not organized as a project *per se*. It is perhaps the case that overall results would not only have been better, but faster and less costly as well—the three classic PM constraints having served their purpose.

The planning, execution, monitoring and control, and closeout (i.e., the project lifecycle) of capital budgets is well-served using PM principles.

Project charter. Some capital projects are so strategic that a sense of fiduciary responsibility alone should compel the most professional approach and set of available techniques. In such cases, it is wise to have a single, clear document that serves little other purpose than to provide the *official* authorization to begin a project, deploy resources, and begin work. Such things should not be ambiguous, not the least of which is investor interest.

Some capital projects warrant their own mission statements, and the kind of matter that appears atop a strategic plan. The project charter may be thought of as an elaboration of a complete mission statement, complete with strategic objectives.

The project charter is normally a separate document a few pages long, articulating: (PMI-PMBOK 2017):

Project purpose or justification, including financial goals;
Business needs, including a high-level project description or business
  proposition;

Measurable requirements that satisfy customer, sponsor, and other stakeholder needs;

Initial project Scope Statement which at least implies the major project deliverables;

Assigned Project Manager and the key team members;

Summary budget and milestone schedule;

Organizational, environmental and external assumptions and constraints.

To emphasize the point about its strategic relevance, a charter is normally signed by the principals, though, of course, the legal implications of that would be more limited than a signature on any legal contract. A legal contract, remember, involves the delivery of a good or service for some form of compensation, monetary or otherwise. As long as all signatories agree on terms, free of duress, there is not much more to the legality of what constitutes a valid contract.

Statement of work (SOW). In the logical flow, next comes a statement of work. *According to the PMBOK, this is "a narrative description of products, services, or results to be supplied."* The SOW should be plainly derivative of the charter, and almost painfully so. Altogether, the SOW defines the scope of the project, and remember, scope is one of the major constraints of any project. *Whether or not the SOW contains a clear and summary scope statement (which is common) and then proceeds to elaborate about it, by its nature, the SOW circumscribes a project scope.* A typical SOW is many pages long, but at the same time, is extremely concise and succinct for the sake of clarity alone.

As to the elaboration of project scope, the typical SOW contains a carefully numbered hierarchy of short pithy paragraphs that have the effect (as well as an eerie feeling) of a contract. A main purpose of the numbering scheme is for quick cross-referencing among legally and contractually important documents; then, as the logic continues, down to individual schedule and budget line-items, earned value management (below), and even job descriptions of key team contributors. It is not too much to expect every member of the project organization to know exactly what paragraph(s) of the SOW one is working on, if, for no other reason, so that the person understands the scope of what labors are to be expected and what would be *out of scope*. This expression is common and is a guiding star used for many purposes.

PM plan. In between writing a project proposal and a project plan, there may be additional documents required beyond a charter and a SOW, but the main points have been made. An understated point aforementioned is that external stakeholders, like investors of capital, need to be considered up front. *The project plan is more utilitarian perhaps; it is referenced and used every day for proper execution, monitoring control, and so on throughout the project lifecycle. The "baseline" plan is a term that refers not to the original plan, but the most recent, formal, and official plan, as it will probably be revised from time to time.* It is the current plan that reflects the present, updated scope and so forth.

Therefore, it is wise to assign some meaningful, dedicated effort for its maintenance and coordination. An obsession with *the plan* can certainly become counterproductive when innovation is part of the scope of a project—a major theme that runs throughout this book in fact—but legal and stakeholder issues at least need satisfaction.

If it has not been articulated as yet, near the top of the project plan is a clear scope statement, often accompanied by a list of major deliverables, outcomes, or requirements. Such things should be written in measurable terms, at least definite enough to enable further translation into contractual and engineering specifications, quality assurance parameters, and perhaps most importantly, customer sign-off and acceptance criteria at time of closeout.

Developing estimates of project returns, that is, free cash flow and all that it entails, is highly dependent on the articulation of the scope.

Project Scope

Managing the project scope, not just articulating one, is one of the main PM knowledge areas. The PMBOK defines scope as *"the work that must be performed to deliver a product, service, or result with the specified features and functions."*

Another important word is deliverables: "Any unique and verifiable product, result or capability to perform a service [internal to the project or to the end-user] that must be produced to complete a process, phase, or product." The word deliverable is part of everyday PM jargon, at every level and by most people. Partly, this is because *deliverables are major contractual outcomes* that also serve as the basis for schedules, budgets, quality goals, and so on.

A deliverable is something that can be measured and quantified as being delivered to that measure. The measure can be something entirely unique such as a design (engineering) specification, or perhaps a simple reference to a broad ISO quality standard (especially for processes), or anything in between. *Here, the allusion to technology standards and dominant designs is intentional.* As such, the deliverable description should provide guidance as to monitoring and control throughout the project, and legal or contractual sign-off at project closeout.

Project scope statement. The *project scope statement* serves as an important referent over the project lifecycle, whereas previously mentioned scope descriptions are somewhat more abstract and only need to serve the purpose of the immediate document. The project charter, for example, is mainly used as the official documentation for project approval and authorization to deploy resources, so the scope description there only needs to be enough for that purpose. In the project plan, more is generally needed in order to provide ongoing guidance to just about any project stakeholder. It is the initial arbiter of misunderstandings about what is in scope, and what is not. It should be updated and officially revised along with other *living* management tools like the baseline plan.

Work breakdown structure. *One might think of a work breakdown structure (WBS) as an exact derivative of the project scope statement, fully elaborated and in a hierarchical format.* Before continuing, however, it is important to realize that the WBS bears no necessary connection to the organization chart, an important subtlety in the following definition: "*A deliverable-oriented hierarchical decomposition of the work to be executed* ... The WBS is decomposed into Work Packages. The deliverable orientation of the hierarchy includes both internal [process capabilities] and external [end-user] deliverables." If the WBS seems a bit inconvenient, that is, if the formal organization chart differs and will create work flow issues, then the organization chart should best be modified, not the WBS. Of course, this is not always practical, so there are ways to handle this. At a high level of organization, there are methods such as the matrix approach described earlier. At lower levels of organization, especially when the time comes to assign duties to specific individuals, there are tools like the responsibility assignment matrix, described later.

It is important to develop the WBS to explicate the scope statement, as it has been articulated into a set of deliverables. A WBS is not an organization chart per se.

That said, a *work package* is: "*A deliverable or project work component at the lowest level of each branch of the Work Breakdown Structure. The Work Package includes the Schedule Activities and Schedule Milestones required to complete the Work package deliverable or project work component.*" Here is further convincing about how important it is to maintain the organization of the WBS, not the organization of the firm. *The full litany of work packages becomes the lowest level of "line items" on budgets and schedules.* If one wants a workable schedule and budget, it is clearly better to maintain a tight accordance with the unique set of deliverables, and not just mimic the standing administrative structure of the local departments.

Hypothetically, *GigaRobots* suggests an imaginary, dedicated, managed project of installing robots at the Tesla Gigafactory. Emphasis on production, not product development, is intentional because of the plight that Tesla got itself into by Musk's own admission—"we were

---

Exhibit 5.1 Simple Work Breakdown Structure

WBS: Project GigaRobots

1.0 Project GigaRobots

    1.1 Deliverable A: Procurement and acquisition

        1.1.1 Work package 1

        1.1.2 Work package 2

        1.1.3 Work package 3

    1.2 Deliverable B: Installation and checkout

        1.2.1 Work package 4

        1.2.2 Work package 5

        1.2.3 Work package 6

        1.2.4 Work package 7

    1.3 Deliverable C: Operational transition and training

        1.3.1 Work package 8

        1.3.2 Work package 9

idiots." Now, it must be admitted that enormous external pressures on Tesla did emphasize production totals over productivity, so things like *Project GigaRobots* would not get priority in such an environment. But a team dedication to such a project might at least keep new capital equipment from being hung from the ceilings as a temporary fix, as happened at Fremont!

Apart from that, these discussions consider capital projects that can be so large, and be so long lasting, that a unique organization must be created and maintained anyway. In that case, as they will both come and go with the fortunes of the project, there is more opportunity to set the *project* organization chart so be so customer-oriented, that it looks much like the WBS. In that case, a project-specific *organizational breakdown structure (OBS) is "A hierarchically organized depiction of the project organization arranged as to regulate the work packages to the performing organizational units."* Now, perhaps, building the entire Gigafactory may enable a clear picture of a distinct capital project that (again, hypothetically) might be funded by, say, a separate bond issue. For example, preparing the property, building the plant, and installing the equipment (the capital PPE on a balance sheet, not coincidentally) intuitively lends itself to an identity of WBS and OBS, where at least identical budget management provides transparency that serves all stakeholders.

This leads naturally to the consideration of scheduling.

Project Schedule

Managing schedules is a major contribution of the PM profession, and one might say "is where it all began" with Henry Gannt, a disciple of Frederick Taylor over 100 years ago during the "Scientific Management" era of the Industrial Revolution.

We still have many charts from those days that Henry Gannt invented and perfected. Today, computerized tools such as PERT and the critical path method, resource loading and balancing, buffering techniques in the resources constraint theory, *fast-tracking* and *slack* reallocation, and integration with budget tracking, are all advanced in the PM lexicon. There are plenty of available software tools to help, including server-based capabilities for managing many projects at once—*perhaps as portfolios.* The implications for managing PM organizations (PMOs) and corporate strategy should be obvious.

Delays in capital projects can easily ruin the business propositions promised in proposals because they change cash flows, the time value of moneys, the true cost of capital, and overall financial results. Scheduling uncertainties is a serious risk factor that can ruin project returns for no other reason than the impact on discounting.

Incidentally, this reality illustrates a vitally important *integration task,* that of managing schedule and cost (or capital) constraints together—in a way, as one problem. Investors readily depend on project deadlines to be met on time to gage their own investment risks and results. Related in a very big way to project success at meeting deliverables, there can be serious legal ramifications about statements that provide *guidance* during official and formal quarterly calls. So the *one problem* here, is a legal one:

(Sparks January 03, 2017).

... management had initially expected to deliver 80,000 to 90,000 vehicles in 2016 but ended up reducing its full-year guidance to about 79,000 ...

... Consistently missing its own targets, including management's initial and revised full-year delivery targets and three of its quarterly guidance targets, makes Tesla's plan to go from its current annualized production run rate of 100,000 units to a target of 500,000 units in 2018 difficult to take seriously.

Not very long after articles like this appeared, Tesla was sued for making impossible delivery promises, not just ambitious ones. *It can never be stressed too much that market cap and the price of corporate stock reflect future expectations, not recent results.* The issue at Tesla was not settled by the time of writing, but the suit alone makes the present point, which incurs major moneys just to manage and settle.

Project Cost

After all the discussions about capital, capital investments, costs of capital, and the rest, little needs to be said about the importance of this constraint. Perhaps, a main contribution is simply to place into the PM consciousness at large how important the costs of capital, hurdle and discount rates, and the effects of time itself, are all so influential to generating free cash flow and satisfying the true owners of the capital being deployed.

There is no such thing as "profit" on a project, really; it is all about free cash flow that contributes not only to accounting profit (earnings), but also economic profit, EVA.

Recall when Tesla was really nothing more or less than the project to field what would become the first Roadster. It is hard to imagine something simpler in the present story and context. Even at that time, and even if strict project management had been employed, there would still be an accounting distance between *project* outcomes and overall *company* outcomes. The mere reality that the founders had already *incorporated* assures this as a matter of fact. There is no such thing as project profit, properly understood, and it matters when capital is externally sourced at the least.

Earned value management (EVM). That point stressed again, next, it needs to be said that EVM should not be confused with EVA. The term *earned value* itself bears a difficult connection to the true economic meaning of value (Martinsuo and Killen 2014).

Without trying to connect all the dots between final corporate EVA and project-budget EVM, there is no doubt that good EVM should contribute to EVA. In fact, EVM can be a key value-adding competence in a project integration capability, especially a PMO.

The overall point of EVM is to provide a composite picture of how the three major project constraints are faring, so intuition alone assures this as one of the effects of good EVM. EVM is a bottom-up technique that takes much time and effort.

It has already been noted that the work package is the lowest level of distinction in project budgets and schedules, or at least the lowest level that is needed for EVM. Each package is carefully monitored for

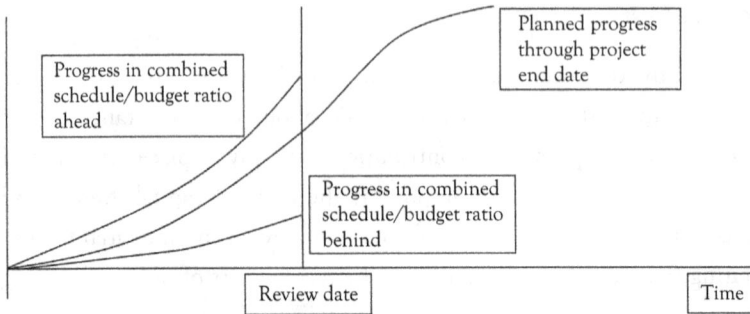

Figure 5.1 EVM summary chart

progress in terms of technical accomplishment and cost, which is one good reason to get a good PM software package. From there, ratios of accomplishment versus costs are constructed, which is another good reason. These are basically *bang for the buck* measures that provide *drill-down* visibility.

As the level of analysis builds from bottom to top, overall indices are created that track progress. These indices are the basis for developing graphical reports used at major review. The following figure provides an example. Its neatness belies all the imaginable *what if's*, of course, once one understands that the curved lines are plots of ratios and indices, constructed from work package data from the bottom-up. See Figure 5.1.

Project Quality

The PMBOK defines quality as *"The degree to which a set of inherent characteristics adheres to a set of requirements"* (PMI-PMBOK 2017). Here the PMI borrows heavily from the corpus of quality management research (Greasley 2006; Heizer and Render 2005; PMI-PMBOK 2017; Stevenson 2009). A main contribution of the PM field is to place quality management tools, techniques, methods, and so on into its overall paradigm of management process flows. The consequences of quality-related problems in new technologies and industries—and companies like Tesla—hardly need explaining, but illustrations help:

(Eisenstein March 30, 2018).

... Tesla is recalling almost half of all the vehicles the company has so far produced, after corroding bolts that could lead to the loss of power steering ...

The service action comes at a particularly inopportune time ... Tesla's stock fell by one-third of its value in recent weeks ... Tesla was buoyed by the sort of stock valuation normally reserved for tech companies like Google and Apple, but investors "were banking on increased earnings ... once they got their manufacturing system fixed. It was going to be a no-brainer."

Now, it must be said that quality management and its set of tools are heavily oriented toward operations that are repetitive, such as in mass manufacturing. Familiar tools include statistical sampling, design of experiments, and control charts. This is excellent as far as it goes, but recall that the definition of a project insists on some level of uniqueness. It is common for a project to only produce something that is *one of a kind*. Countless capital projects serve as cases in point such as, for example, *productizing* the Freemont factory as a manufacturing *dreadnought*. For that matter, anything with the words *first-mover advantage* attached—meaningfully and not blithely attached, that is—must, by definition, be similar.

Most of the capital projects in these discussions imply a significant amount of uniqueness and indeed, true innovation whether it be incremental or discontinuous. In such cases, the risks differ, and this affects investment risk and hurdle rates.

Here, the reader is referred to Volume II for discussions about capital projects as real options. What emerges from this view is a strong need in management itself to develop a combined capability in technology risk management, quality management, and capital project finance. Consider:

(Sparks December 30, 2016).

... Consumer Reports once again named electric-car maker Tesla Motors the most-loved car brand, with the brand's 91% overall owner-satisfaction rating trouncing every other car maker on the planet ...

Tesla's ability to satisfy customers is a key metric for investors. It's crucial for a young automaker to stand out with satisfying products. If Tesla's ability to delight customers fades, its well-capitalized competition could establish a foothold with would-be Tesla customers and mitigate Tesla's growth potential.

Such an accomplishment is unique and does not happen as a matter of course, or as a fortunate happenstance of everyday operations. Still, the Tesla story makes plain that unless something about it *precludes the competition* from doing much the same at reasonable *capital cost* and within a reasonable time frame (to at least catch up), there is no first-mover advantage *per se*. It did not take long for VW, Daimler, Nissan, Toyota, GM, and even SAIC to *come out of nowhere* even in this massively *capital-intense and capital-costly* field.

The double-edged sword of depending exclusively *on high quality is that "the good is the enemy of the best," and even the definition of "best" is always elevating. Quality-based,* time-to-market based profits *are short-lived, unless a firm has the organization wide* capability *of consistently and sustainably being first; this exemplifies* profitability and sustained EVA, and high returns to capital employed.

Project Staffing

Technically, the PMI calls this knowledge area project resources management, though even then the issue is really HR as it directly relates to PM. To be more *avant-garde* about it, though, one might also draw the distinction between intellectual capital and other forms of capital such as money, land, and equipment. That would certainly be in line with the main themes of this series, which all come down to making a return on invested capital in the broader idea of how capitalism works as an economics theory.

No form of capital should take precedence over any other, especially in an information-driven economy. "Intellectual property" is no misnomer in the modern understanding of capitalism.

Anyway, upon inspection most of the project-specific issues seem attuned to the problem of staffing—but throughout the entire project lifecycle, not just the more specific issue of internal or external recruiting. Staffing is a very critical issue as it concerns initial project team formation, but the team composition can easily change over time. As most of the kinds of capital projects considered here are truly multi disciplinary in nature, project managers are themselves constrained to finding a very few people of high competencies in their respective fields. Moreover, the *portfolio of competencies* in any long-term capital project is likely to evolve over the project lifecycle, and for more than the obvious reasons. Consider:

(Olinga January 13, 2016).

... the self-driving, mass-market electric car widely seen as the future of the auto industry -- founder Elon Musk is rapidly staffing up with the best talent he can find: computer programmers.

Rather than look to Detroit for help to build his cars, Musk's 12 year old company is focused on Silicon Valley to recruit some 1,600 software engineers for the next stage ... Crossing into the field with their substantial resources and tech capabilities are Internet giants like Google, Apple, and Uber ... Tesla has a march on the competition; the question is whether it can hold on.

Assuming the preceding recruiting proved successful, each person would seem to be a very valuable asset. How should their work be allocated in a way that precludes competition or their services?

The RAM. Many project team members are formally assigned to more than one project at a time. Not only is getting the *right people* a challenge, then, but getting enough of their time allocated to a project is another. Again, anything approaching matrix management should be accompanied by some training of managers as well as individual team members.

A tool that may help is the responsibility assignment matrix (RAM). See Table 5.1. It shows how individual members of a project team can be assigned to specific roles toward the accomplishment of various work packages and deliverables. One may find the slicing and dicing of roles a bit too fine or impractical in this example, but the idea right now is

Table 5.1 RAM

	Team design engineer (R&D)	Team production engineer (Manufacturing)	Team software engineer (IT)	Project leader
SOW/ WBS/WP 1.1	R	T		I
SOW/ WBS/WP 1.2		R	T	I
SOW/ WBS/WP 1.3	R	I	T	I

Legend: R: Responsible or accountable for deliverable
          T: Technical support
          C: Coordination
          I: Informed

about planning the project HR along with and as part of planning budget, schedule, and the rest. See Table 5.1.

A tool like this can also help initially plan labor as a resource while providing good visibility into who should be doing what as it relates to the lowest-level schedule line-item, budget line-item, and EVM, that is, down to the level of the individual work package, each package subordinate to a deliverable. Once a project is off and running, it is more the case that team members will act smoothly as a unit. Still, things can drift and get confused on long projects, especially if there is turnover, and the RAM can be used to get back on track. In contrast:

(Sage and Rodriguez July 2, 2018).

… Tesla pulled out all the stops in the final week of June to meet its goal of making 5,000 Model 3s in a week …

… Musk paced the Model 3 line, snapping at his engineers when the around-the-clock production slowed or stopped due to problems with robots …

Some employees are worried the frenetic pace plus long hours could burn out workers. One employee said they were told to keep working until they met their daily production mark, not when their shifts ended.

At the latter end of the project lifecycle, there are closeout issues that are not to be mishandled. Assume for the moment that a *Project 5,000* had been organized to accomplish the aforementioned milestone months earlier and that now, *borrowed* people could go back to their *regular jobs* in Nevada and so forth. Or, consider the potential for confusion when it comes time for formal performance appraisals from one's *real* boss:

(Hull March 29, 2018).

Tesla Inc. exhorted its factory workers to disprove the "haters" betting against the company wrong and is *letting a small number of volunteers join the effort* to ramp up output of the crucial Model 3 line ...

[A Tesla employee said] "The world is watching us very closely ... This is a critical moment in Tesla's history, and there are a number of reasons it's so important. You should pick the one that hits you in the gut and makes you want to win."

In some industries, it is not uncommon for the closeout of major capital projects to include layoffs, even when a project has been very successful. In a matrix organization, an individual may at least take solace in the probability that another project is right around the corner, and that one's career contiguity is already in the planning. Project team members and managers alike should take into account that they will probably work with each other again.

Project Risk

The PMBOK (PMI-PMBOK 2017) defines risk as "An uncertain event or condition that, if it occurs, has a positive or negative affect on a project's objectives." First, it is interesting that this definition says that uncertainties can be either positive or negative. As counterintuitive as that might sound at first, it does open the mind in a good way. One immediate practicality is that there are *strategies* for both positive and negative risks.

Second, it helps avoid a common error that is easily fixed with just a few seconds' thought. The error occurs where managing risks becomes confused with managing crises. In an important sense, they are opposite.

Without torturing the obvious, the uncertainty of any event applies to its future, not its present. One might say that when risk management is perfect, crises never occur, but, this is not to say that bad things never occur. It means that the planning has been good enough to keep urgencies manageable short of panic, injury, catastrophic cost, and so on.

A main objective of managing an uncertain future event—in the present—*is to avoid a future crisis from ever occurring.*

Still, despite the best planning, events do occur without enough warning to manage well. Contingency plans, budget set-asides, and scheduled time buffers are often wise to incorporate in plans. However, there is no such contingency called *just in case,* unless *perhaps* one is thinking of a black swan event.

By way of contrast, (a) a black swan in business lingo is an event that could not have been foreseen, a kind of *unknown-unknown* in the jargon, while (b) a random event is one where its probability of occurring is the same as any other alternative possibility, a kind of *known-unknown.*

Even a random event has a *manageable* probability. Lightning strikes and some kinds of auto accidents are examples; for that matter, lightning actually striking an auto is a random event, as opposed to, say, an auto striking a pedestrian versus a telephone pole. It does help to understand this if one has at least a good intuitive sense of probability theory, if not a bit of training. Still, there is an ordinary point to this, soon.

A random event is *not* one where the probability of occurrence is very low for example, *miraculous.* An event is random if its probability is the same as the probability of any other possibility. The flip of a coin is a random event, but after all, the probability of either possibility is a very known, dependable, and *manageable* 50 percent. Guessing *heads* and winning is no miracle, at least not in Vegas.

To apply this lame attempt at whimsy, when it was suddenly (in the media, anyway) realized that there was plenty of lithium in the world, completely reversing the prior expectation of its encroaching rarity due to demands for batteries of many kinds, that was a black swan event to anyone invested in lithium as a commodity (the commodity price plunged). Nobody saw it coming, but we all know *stuff happens* even when it comes completely out of the blue (with apologies, another confusing lightning reference).

In contrast, which battery advancement (or type) would someday replace present-day lithium technology due to the mythical *technological breakthrough* (always rumored to be a year away) should be considered random (as the rumors were so unreliable, and because the number of firms involved was large and yet, because many such efforts were done quietly, if not secretly).

Now, imagine yourself being a project risk manager at an auto firm. There, *just in case* is not a tool, it is a short cut. It should be plain that managing a *future* black swan, *now*, is still not only a possibility, but a responsibility. However, its *nature* requires a different tool than events that have estimable probabilities, to include random events, where methods like actuarial analysis serve well historically.

"Risky" events differ in their basic (e.g., probabilistic) natures, *first and foremost, not just their* kinds *(e.g., financial versus schedule).*

Now, more for general interest, intuitive closure can be reached on an earlier point. A contingency reserve is not a *slush fund*. Such thinking really applies to black swans, and black swans are not contingencies. Contingencies are known to happen, even if they happen randomly. In contrast, *slack* in schedules or anything else (here, budgets) applies to managing probabilistic contingencies.

Slack is a valuable resource, not a waste of time; the idea applies to slack of all kinds. It is a matter of project efficiency and the productivity, hence profitability, of capital.

The summary point is that it matters to proper risk management that the proper tool be applied to the *nature* of the problem, not just the *kind*. There are different tools and techniques for assessing each in the very broadly dispersed risk management literature. There is no single scholarly corpus covering all the possibilities, so readers are invited to explore their fields.

Financial risk is one kind, though it can then be understood as being characterized by the *natures* of various subcategories. For example, to a financier used to Capital Asset Planning Model methodology (Volume II), systematic asset risk is not the same in nature as inflation risk, though they are both measured in compatible ways, and can literally be added to determine a discount rate. More broadly, later discussions in this series outline how to handle the investment risks due to the nature of capital projects, building from scratch starting, say, by considering the time value of money, namely, the risk-free rates of government treasuries, to adopting complex asset pricing models for managing whole project phases as financial options. There are whole categories of other risks to consider, but they all relate to investment risk in the end: technology risk, political risk, market risk, economic risk, ... not to mention the competition. Consider:

(McLaughlin August 14, 2015).

... Tesla isn't just building cars; it is also building a vertically integrated supply chain and a proprietary recharging network ... greater investment is required by Tesla to build these multiple businesses simultaneously. Tesla is ... burning cash as a company to make these major investments.

Tesla's path to profitability relies on harnessing the multiple reinforcing feedbacks to bring down battery costs rapidly and grow the global market for electric vehicles. Growth in Tesla sales will accelerate the accumulation of production experience, realize economies of scale in manufacturing.

That article sums up the entire Tesla story about as well as any other, and the one thing that leaps out at the reader is the complexity, not just the enormity, of the risk(s). Certainly, a rational method of sorting it out should help. There are several.

The most common rubric for managing risk is to imagine future events along two dimensions. First, and as one should expect at this point, there is the actual, statistical probability of the uncertain future event occurring. Second is the qualitatively assessed impact of the event should it occur at all.

The risk *of a* future uncertainty, to be managed today, *is the probability* × *the impact.*

Of course, it is technically impossible to multiply a probability times a qualitative measure and get one number, but this is beside the present point. The two basic parameters are often considered to be two orthogonal axes (independent of each other in principle), which is commonly illustrated by using a matrix like the one shown next. What has been added here are the boldfaced risk strategies or policies in the *boxes*.

Table 5.2 Probability-impact matrix and policy responses

	Safety effect	Operational effect	Maintenance effect
High probability of failure (poor reliability)	High risk *Policy: Avoid*		Mixed *Policy: Mitigate*
		Revenue effect *Policy: Warranty*	
Low probability of failure (good reliability)	Mixed *Policy: Mitigate*		Low risk *Policy: Let fail*

For example, if during the design stage of an important subsystem component, an engineer, safety analyst, or the like realizes that all the suitable components available from suppliers have worrisome reliability histories, and that if the component should fail, there will be injuries, then the obvious strategy is to do something at that point to disallow it from ever happening. In such an instance, the understated word for this a policy (see the table 5.2) is *avoid*. Options include, on the probability side, reducing the likelihood to near-zero, say, by designing a superior component internally with much better reliability, or, on the impact side, change the effect by designing a *fail-safe* feature, such that when the component fails, it does so without anybody getting hurt—by design. Either solution is adequate in terms of the word *avoid* and compliance with its inferred policy.

At the other corner of the matrix, assume that the same, superior component will also be used in another subsystem, where it will have a low probability of failure, and when it does fail, there is no meaningful immediate effect. By policy, as a matter of planning that is, the economically best thing to do about the system design is nothing, except perhaps to make sure the component can be readily and economically repaired or replaced.

As disturbing as it may seem to the novice to just *let* things fail as a matter of planning, one can observe that many, if not most, failures in life are managed in much the same way. Controversies surrounding preventive health care and its insurance provide a sterling example. One does not *plan to fail,* but *failing to plan* is another thing entirely. Once more, we see the management of constraint trade-offs emerging as a real competence across-the-board.

The nature *of failure is handled by* a policy *consequent to its* overall risk. *The matrix is* not an *ex post* diagnostic tool, *it is an ex ante, policy determination aid.*

Procurement and Contracting

The importance of supply chains surfaced over and again in the Tesla story, from the very beginning with the relationships with ACPropulsion and Lotus, to the last when Musk complained publicly to investors that the company needed to regain control of its many contractors for cash flow purposes alone. Especially in the kind of capital projects being considered, managing supply chains is of paramount importance from the standpoint of finding, certifying, and bargaining with contractors, to determining the number and nature of collaborative relationships, to vertical integration and outsourcing strategy, on and on down to include the need to handmade components during the final assembly stage. Also, the acquisition of capital equipment (not just vehicle parts, and not just whole companies and Gigafactories) was in the balance. When it all comes down to it, everything, except the purest service, is logistical.

(Stafford April 14, 2016).

Demand for lithium ... is poised to continue on its upward trajectory, becoming the world's new gasoline and earning the moniker of "White Petroleum" ...

"In order to produce a half million cars per year…we would basically need to absorb the entire world's lithium-ion production" ... Tesla's soon-to-be-completed gigafactory will produce more lithium-ion batteries than the rest of the world combined.

Because the procurement and contracting function is the one that directly interfaces with external providers, there is scant room for sloppiness. Not only is cost at immediate issue, but so are many legal considerations. Consider:

(McKenna July 24, 2018).

...

By

REPORTER
the company is focused on reaching a "more sustainable" long-term
cost basis with suppliers. ... Any changes with suppliers would improve
Tesla's future cash flows "but not impact our ability to achieve profitability in Q3," ... Discussions with suppliers are focused entirely on
future parts price and design or process changes ... intended to lower
costs in the future rather than make prior period adjustments of capital
expenditure projects.

A great deal of work is generally needed just to identify qualified suppliers, and legal statutes governing the fairness of these processes exist at
all levels of jurisdiction. There are also industry-specific standards and of
course, international. The bidding process itself can be quite rule-bound,
and here is where contracting people often refer to RFPs, which stands for
request for proposal, an important precursor to letting a final contract for
important and costly things. The issue not only about raw materials, but
property, plant, and capital equipment—the PP&E that appears first as
fixed assets on balance sheets, and which constitutes the majority of the
investment capital in many cases.

There is no more important business function than procurement and
contracting toward making positive free cash flow at the project level, and
EVA at the corporate level. This is where the economic theory turns into
final numbers on the cost side of the equation, at least. Luckily, there is no
shortage of literature on the matter, and there are many fine professional
associations to contact. Many are industry- or profession specific.

Project Communications and Stakeholder Management

Because of their elevated importance in the Tesla saga, these knowledge
areas were addressed in the previous chapter.

Conclusion

This chapter complements other chapters and volumes in the series by explaining the basics of PM as guided by the PMI and the PMBOK. The PMI is generally considered to be the global thought leader in this field.

PM is broken out into areas of knowledge, where each can be likened to a managerial competency. *Altogether and when managed using portfolio and PMO concepts, it becomes a viable* capability *and basis* for competitive advantage.

The discussion was framed in the more specific context of managing capital projects that are found in capital budgets and are subject to the capital budgeting process exercised in most corporations, whether single-industry or multidivisional. The Tesla saga was extended as an illustrative case study.

Discussion Questions

Referencing any organization of choice, how could a PM approach help manage capital projects individually and in portfolios?

Continuing the aforementioned, what is the relative importance of the knowledge areas as they relate to managing capital projects?

Exercises

Continuing the aforementioned, diagram a project-oriented organization chart, and discuss the pros and cons of your decisions.

Continuing the aforementioned, circumscribe one major capital project, identify its major constraints, and note the consequent trade-offs among them.

Continuing the aforementioned, outline its scope, charter, SOW, deliverables, and devise a top-level WBS.

CHAPTER 6

Epilogue and Conclusion

Introduction

During the early years at Tesla, it was a design company, a component or subsystem supplier, in some ways a typical Silicon Valley technology entrepreneurship. In order to manufacture all-battery electric vehicles (EVs) of mass-market viability, however, it needed to become another kind of company, more like the traditional system integrator, an original equipment manufacturer (OEM) in the key position in a complex and extensive supply chain, one that went all the way from raw supplies of lithium and cobalt, to a utilities-like manager of recharging infrastructure.

However, it could prove pathological if, in the pursuit of scale and mass-markets, Tesla returned to an obsolete, top-down, risk-averse, and arguably, un-innovative bygone era. The organization form and function would prove instrumental, not just technology and marketing.

Also, some of Elon Musk's communications and style were becoming quite concerning, suggesting the need for executive succession at the very top. This is said only to point to the trauma it would cause to the entire corporation. Just reviewing events to as recently as possible suggests that something had to happen.

After Studying this Chapter, the Reader will be Able to Discuss

The need to *anticipate and enact* an organizational transition as external conditions evolve.

How different corporate strategies translate to specific areas of project risk.

Whether a project management organization (PMO) or portfolio might beat the *technological breakthrough* myth.

Co-Evolution of Industries and Firms

Tesla incorporated at about the same time it became obvious how much capital it would take to become the first manufacturer of commercially viable all-battery EVs. Yet, even this accomplishment was not as great as the ambition of doing all this for the global mass market, *en route* to saving the planet. It was not just a question of market *size* and related economies of scale and scope, it was also a question of satisfying evolving market demand *characteristics.*

First, unit prices had to come down very considerably—say, on the order of 25–50 percent. Second, but at the same time, range (and recharging convenience) would still dominate purchasing decisions. Third, on the other hand, consumer priorities were beginning to shift as market niches and segments advanced. In addition to being price-sensitive, mass markets consider things like: reliability (i.e., what *quality* becomes); replacement battery costs (tens of thousands of dollars) and hardware upgrades (e.g., autopilot); and in a few words, total cost of ownership (resale, subsidy effects, home power upgrades, costs of recharging). *Sizzle* may still be the order of the day for technophiles and wealthy environmentalists, but the more pragmatic mass market expects high quality at good prices, and is able to tell the difference. It cannot be said that the EV industry was approaching *technological* maturity, but *demand* characteristics were starting to show signs of change.

For the moment, stick with the latter notion. As an industry approaches maturity, the key is to successfully navigate the treacherous *transition* period; afterward, things become relatively stable. Being proactively engaged in encroaching market saturation is a significant challenge, and failing at it has caused the demise of countless firms. It often starts by the players themselves of collective over-investment during a period of optimistic growth. This shoots collective production capacity above the collective market demand, and shakeouts occur (Grant 2002; Porter 1980).

Overcapacity is one result of mistiming slowing market growth, plus underestimating similar expansion plays made by the competition, and triggers desperate strategies.

Sooner or later, the demand flattens, and that is a treacherous problem, as Wall Street is unrelenting about growth imperatives. If firms want to grow in a mature, saturated market, where firms survive based on repeat purchases made by sophisticated consumers, it means they need to wrest market share from each other. Marketing efforts emphasize repeat purchasers. Price wars are common just to sustain production economics. Self-destructive tactics often ensue to preserve market share (by slashing prices) to maintain economies of scale. The innovation emphasis shifts to incrementally improved, high-quality products produced at low unit cost.

Some players who never had a good strategy become desperate to the point of embarrassment. Meanwhile, consumers might vainly hope for a technological breakthrough.

Eventually, there is not enough *profitable* business to go around, and the bubble bursts. It may be time to completely abandon attempts at major product enhancements. It may be time to only improve the product if it helps to improve processes, quite a reversal from earlier phases. Short of making a jump to another product technology, a focus on process (e.g., manufacturing) technologies becomes the focus, where capital investments are more likely to make thin-but-positive, that is, acceptable returns considering the risks.

Thus, a poorly anticipated transition to maturity can be strategically catastrophic, and this includes the transition of an organization to fit best with the changing environment.

It is the *anticipation* that matters. Tesla needed professional management—but on the order of which profession?

Through 1Q 2019: A Work in Progress

As 2018 turned into 2019, here are some facts and figures concerning Tesla and EVs more generally (Eisenstein 2019):

- Tesla had 83 percent of the *battery-only* EV market share in the United States;
- As much as 200 billion U.S. dollars could be spent on *all*-battery EVs in the coming decade;
- The totals were still small compared to the global market for all autos and was only 4 percent of the Chinese market;
- By 2022, 207 EV models were projected to be on the roads; and
- By 2023, 225 billion U.S. dollars would be spent on combined EV R&D; altogether.

This section follows events of the time chronologically, and at the same time, divides things according to the major kind of risk.

Capital Risk

In the final month of 2018, the entire stock market had experienced a crash of its own, that in the early months of 2019 began to revive, but not without some nervous trepidation. From the perspective on Wall Street, much of the first quarter news about Tesla was just a continuation of the expectations that closed out 2018. One thing that became thematic in the media was that demand for *Tesla* EVs *specifically* looked to be weakening. While the previous problem was making enough cars to meet demand, stay ahead of the competition, honor car down-payments, and beat the expiration of tax benefits, now the danger of not having enough customers in the first place became a concern. At least, Tesla cut vehicle prices by several thousand dollars at a time it could hardly spare the cash.

Meanwhile, driven by popular appeal and a surge in the ability of the United States to provide of its own energy, demand for regular *cars* waned—but was partly replaced by a surge in demand for pickup trucks and SUVs. Also, considering all the announcements made across the global industry, overcapacity of vehicles and batteries types seemed inevitable:

(Eisentstain January 31, 2019).

close dialog

… vehicles using all the various forms of electrified powertrain technologies — including conventional hybrids — will reach the "tipping point," early in the 2020s …

…"It's going to be a battle" out there … especially in the next five years. Declining costs, longer range, the increased availability of fast chargers and other factors may eventually help win buyers over to EVs. But, for now, almost everyone seems to agree that plugging in will be, despite Musk's enthusiasm, a recipe for losing money.

Procurement Risk

This was a time when the trade war with China, as well in the EU and NAFTA, seemed to make progress and then, degenerate quickly. Tariffs on steel and aluminum were continued, despite loud calls from industries like auto, but later were revoked to stoke the chances of *NAFTA 2.0* being ratified by the respective three governments. This was important first, because of the component cost of steel and aluminum in all autos; secondly, the massively complex auto supply chains across all borders; and third, the import-export costs of whole autos themselves. The tariffs cost GM and Ford each one billion U.S. dollars in just a portion of 2018. In a matter of months, the *trade* war shifted emphasis from things like the current account (*balance of trade*) and job losses to intellectual property—*forced* technology transfer as a condition for market entry, and the much more insidious issue of intellectual property theft.

(Krishner January 03, 2019).

… one [Model Y] production location is known: the *Tesla Gigafactory 3* in Shanghai … All of the vehicles produced [there, including Model 3] will be built for the Chinese market …

... the Fremont, Calif., car factory is maxed out with Model 3 production, and Gigafactory 1 in Nevada isn't fit for auto production (without expensive upgrades), so it's possible that the production for the rest of the world could be switched to a Tesla factory in Europe ...

As for production itself, Musk claims the Model Y will bring a "manufacturing revolution" in 2020. Much of this has to do with *fixing mistakes the company made in producing the Model 3*.

Procurement risk rose to the highest strategic levels. Tesla's moves regarding China had more the appearance of what academics call a *multidomestic* or *multinational* strategy; the point of which is to not only produce where the markets are, but also source locally.

As far as practical, in a multidomestic strategy, each market's supply chain would be self-contained and self-serving. Procurement risks vary accordingly.

Scale was achieved through networks, consortia, partnerships, and the like, which in turn were innovating new means of financing high-tech ventures. Even technology development develops locally in many cases. Science itself is no longer the exclusive province of advanced countries with the best university systems and traditional corporate powerhouses.

In a matter of months, the *trade* war shifted emphasis from things like the current account (*balance of trade*) and job gains and losses, to intellectual property—*forced* technology transfer as a condition for market entry, and the different and much more insidious issue of intellectual property theft. A more multinational approach would thus obviate the trade tensions that were dividing up the world that way anyway:

(Shepardson January 4, 2019).

Tesla Inc. has asked the Trump administration to exempt the Chinese-made car computer "brain" of its new Model 3 sedan from 25 percent tariffs imposed in August ...

Tesla ... added that "choosing any other supplier would have delayed the (Model 3) program by 18 months with clean room setup, line validation, and staff training."

Using a new supplier "substantially increases the risk of poor part quality that could lead overall vehicle quality issues that would impact the safety of our vehicles and the consumer acceptance."

A few days later:

(No author January 06, 2019).

... Tesla Inc. is finally breaking ground on its $5 billion factory in the world's biggest auto market ...

A fully owned facility also would mean Tesla won't need to share its profits and technology with Chinese partners, unlike other foreign carmakers who are required to form a domestic joint venture.

Domestic production would help shield Tesla against import duties as the U.S. and China find ways to wriggle out of the tariff quandary.

The most obvious downside of a multinational strategy in the new era is the sacrifice of some global economies of scale, but after all, China was by far the largest EV market in the world with scale economies all its own that would *subsidize* unit costs globally. As well, robotics, artificial intelligence, and other production advances were continuing to change the very nature of parameters like facility capacity, economies of scope, and so forth.

In contrast, a true *global strategy* means much more than just doing business all over the world. A global strategy views the entire world as one market, where products can be standardized as much as possible, in turn aiming to consolidate as much as possible where production scale can be maximized, with supply chains structured with as little regard to political boundaries as possible.

Altogether, in the present story, more sensible hybrid strategies were seeking to optimize the pros and cons of global scale versus local responsiveness. *Pure* strategies of any kind are generally difficult in such a complex and dynamic world.

Technology Risk

First, General Motors seemed to be taking the challenge even more seriously than it had prior. Despite the more famous Volt and Bolt, much of its EV strategy seemed focused on institutional markets for autonomous vehicles and altogether, compliance with regulations at all levels. Still, early in 2019, it made an announcement that finally seemed directly responsive to Tesla:

(Shepardson January 10, 2019).

… a Cadillac will be the first vehicle based on its forthcoming "BEV3" platform … the basis for vehicle underpinnings, including the battery system and other structural and mechanical parts …

… [CEO] Barra has said that GM aims to sell 1 million electric vehicles a year by 2026, many of them in China, which has set strict production quotas on such vehicles.

Several days later, with a bit more drama:

(Carey, and White January 14, 2019).

General Motors Co.'s strategy to make its luxury Cadillac marque its lead electric vehicle brand is the automaker's final opportunity to turn the unit around and make it a success …

[The official] did not elaborate on what would happen if the multiyear effort to make the Cadillac brand more profitable failed …

… [He] said "one of the first" fully electric Cadillac models using the new platform would be on the market around 2022.

Second, but related, even as small as the EV market still was as a percentage of the whole, the availability of recharging solutions was not keeping up. In 2019, the global EV fleet reached million cars, and there were 632,000 public charging outlets worldwide. It was forecast that between 14 and 30 million would be needed by 2030 (Eckhouse, Stringer and Hodges 2019). This assumes EVs would reach 30 percent of the global market share. Clearly, the U.S. EV industry was not going to be determined by a battle between two American companies, Tesla and GM. It was possible—through very unlikely given their savvy—that either one or both could be locked out!

In the commercial evolution of markets and industries, there is no greater technology risk than being locked out of technology standards and dominant designs.

It was still far from true that any charger would do the trick for any EV owner under any of a set of common conditions. Some chargers provided only 10 miles of range for 30 minutes of charge time. Regular household power could need 12 hours to charge from 20 percent back to full charge, in effect overnight. In the middle, some roadside chargers could provide 10–60 miles of range in a 60-minute charge. Fast chargers could provide 75 miles in 30 minutes, and of course, was most expensive; eight charges a day would reach the breakeven point for each charger:

(Eckhouse, Stringer and Hodges February 17, 2019).

... An alliance of Volkswagen AG, Daimler AG, Ford Motor Co. and BMW AG ... plans to build a total of 400 charging stations across Europe by next year ...

Volkswagen's Electrify America unit plans to spend $2 billion ... $800 million in California ... it had 105 electric-vehicle charging sites in the U.S. and plans to have 484 built by July 1 ...

[But] Charging network operators need to prepare for new consumers in the next decade who'll be less tolerant than early adopters ...

For EVs to go from "crazy boutique small to mainstream," the industry needs cheaper vehicles that can drive further on a single charge ... "there has to be charging infrastructure everywhere."

However, the *growth* problem now was about *standardization* as much as recharging time. In the United States, there were still three charging standards, and within each, payment schemes varied. One competing standard was Tesla's, which already had 12,000 chargers at over 1,400 sites worldwide, including China. China had one standard, mandated by the government. In the United States, auto makers were playing a larger role than in other countries where governments were more active, though state governments continued to vary greatly in their support. At any rate, Tesla's massive capital investments hinged on delivering EVs that must be compatible with the recharging standard in China. But, the three standards that already existed in the United States were largely being resolved by depending on market forces, which do not, history shows, always pick the *best* technology.

Mass markets demand dependability, of both the companies they patronize and enough product technology predictability that their decisions will not suddenly become obsolete.

Competing products do not need to be functionally identical (which would work against differentiation anyway), but they should at least be technologically compatible (and perhaps create network externalities). Therefore, overall mass-market growth itself is often inhibited by a lack of technology standards and a dominant design.

Contracting Risk

VW had announced great EV plans, but it did not plan on going alone. Of course, it must be said that some of it was a result of VW's settlement with the U.S. government over an egregious emissions-monitoring software scandal. On the other hand, WV already targeted becoming completely carbon-free by the year 2050, so perhaps motives did not matter much. The news brought Tesla—otherwise a clear nemesis—into their emerging business ecosystem:

(McGee February 4, 2019).

Volkswagen will purchase and install more than 100 Powerpack battery recharging stations from Tesla in the US this year, as it rolls out infrastructure for the coming wave of electric cars.

… "Tesla's Powerpack system is a natural fit given their global expertise in both battery storage development and EV charging" …

...Volkswagen is also beginning mass production next year of a giant "powerbank" designed to charge electric cars at places where infrastructure is lacking, such as concerts and other large-scale events.

Then, again:

(No author March 4, 2019).

Volkswagen has signed German start-up e.GO Mobile as the first external partner for its modular platform for electric vehicles (EV), as it seeks to simplify production ...

The platform seeks the cost advantages of large production numbers by standardizing as much as possible even across very different models.

Volkswagen ... said it was exploring joint development of e-vehicles with Ford, under a wide-ranging partnership ...

The carmaker's electric-vehicle investment budget outstrips that of its closest competitors, in pursuit of profitable mass-production of electric vehicles.

And:

(Whitley and Behrmann March 7, 2019).

... By doubling power at Tesla's stations ... charging times will drop to around 15 minutes ...

... After debuting in North America, the [V3] technology will reach Europe and the Asia-Pacific region in the fourth quarter ...

... The company is looking to ward off a wave of [recharging] competition from ... Ionity GmbH, a consortium of Volkswagen AG, Mercedes Benz-maker Daimler AG, Ford Motor Co. and BMW AG, [which] will have 400 station across Europe's major highways ....

VW-owned brand Porsche ... is also adding 350 kW chargers to its dealerships in the U.S. and Europe.

And as if the reminder was necessary:

(Taylor March 13, 2019).

... The company plans to become the world's biggest producer of electric cars by 2025, with the VW brand alone aiming to build more than 20 models on the group's electric vehicles platform ...

VW will start building the ID [first platform model] at a factory in Zwickau, Germany, which has maximum annual production capacity of 330,000 models. Zwickau will also build electric cars for Volkswagen's Seat and Audi brands.

After Zwickau, Volkswagen will roll out production of electric vehicles to seven other factories worldwide including two plants in China and a factory in Chattanooga, United States, VW said.

Or, in other words, VW was content to partner with Tesla about some of its recharging issues, but in a limited fashion, and no doubt, politically motivated. Given Tesla's history and Musk's personality, perhaps that was entirely suitable—even for the best. VW seemed to have its hand in everything, and it was clearly hedging its bets when it came to battery technology, as well as higher-level issues.

In an era of rapidly shifting alliances, managing contracting risk should also consider the pass-through of intellectual property to third parties.

Dropping down a level of analysis—to *batteries* that is—much the same story continued:

(Frangoul March 8, 2019).

[While] Japanese car giant Nissan says its compact hatchback called Leaf has become the first electric car to exceed 400,000 in sales ...

Volvo Group Venture Capital, a subsidiary of the Volvo Group, invested in a company that specializes in the "high power wireless charging of electric vehicles."

The wireless charging business, called Momentum Dynamics, is based in Pennsylvania. It is developing and commercializing "high power inductive charging for the automotive and transportation industries."

VW was never far from the conversation:

(Scheyder March 12, 2019).

… Ford has also announced a commercial vehicle alliance with Germany's Volkswagen AG, with plans to jointly develop electric and self-driving vehicles …

… it is considering forging supply deals with lithium producers, Ford said …

Ford rival Tesla Inc. has a lithium supply deal with Australia's Kidman Resources Ltd.

"We are looking at the entire supply chain and where we want to play" … Albemarle Corp and SQM are the world's largest lithium producers.

Although

(Zaleski March 17, 2019).

… "Lithium is pretty much hitting a wall right now. If you really want to increase energy density, you have to go to a completely different paradigm" …

…. Starting this year, several start-ups with batteries they believe are big improvements over current lithium-ion technology will introduce their cells to the commercial market.

"It's taken us eight years and probably 35,000 iterations of our material synthesis just to have something that's commercially ready" ….

… about 10 years of research. Only now are start-ups gearing up for the commercial spotlight, a rollout that will take at least a few years, and possibly even another full decade.

Like several others like it, that article went on to discuss solid-state battery technology being developed by a promising start-up. VW was again involved, with a 100 million U.S. dollar investment. The new battery might increase the range of the VW E-Golf from 186 to 466 miles, and competitive with gas model ranges. If true, that would be a stupendous jump in range, anyway.

However, these observations are typical of the mirage called "technological breakthrough."

An interesting quip came from one of the principles:

> The long development timeline for these start-ups is a sign of how difficult pushing battery technology can be ... You're talking about a generational technological shift that has to happen ... In 150 years of batteries existing, there have been four commercially relevant chemistries to come to market. And every time you go to these new chemistries, they get harder (Zaleski 2019).

Critique: The Ultimate Deliverable

It is difficult to pick just one kind of risk that the rest of the period depicts, so perhaps it all comes down to managing integration and scope.

In the middle of the first quarter, Tesla announced long awaited and happy news. To this point, Tesla had been making the Model 3, delivering 145,610 in fact, but still priced much too high. With a base range of 220 miles:

(Ferris and Kopecki February 28, 2019).

... Tesla is finally launching its long-awaited standard Model 3 starting at $35,000 ...

We think it's a mistake from a strategic perspective and are skeptical of the gross margins on that $35,000 vehicle. In our view, they would be better served sticking to premium electric vehicles instead of this mass market, Henry Ford-type mentality of affordable vehicles for all.

... It might be different if Tesla had the production capacity to drive volume and margin for this lower priced version, but they don't currently and to add the incremental capacity would require significant additional capital investment.

That represented the major deliverable: a viable mass-marketable all-battery EV. But, free cash flow (FCF) and EVA were certainly negative, and deadlines were missed. In addition to the obvious, discounting effects on cash flow and the cost of capital amplify the point about deadlines.

With that, Musk admitted to structurally obstinate cost problems, and that the company would not be announcing a quarterly (accounting) profit. He had hopes for sustained profitability afterward, but of course, he always did. Evidently and by Musk's own admission, the mass-market Model 3 was now a consumer reality, but the business model it represented was still not sustainably profitable in real economic terms. Yet, there was no sign of slowing the firm's expansion goals.

Conclusion

The purpose of this chapter was to help all sides of the controversy about the need for Tesla to become more professionally managed or in kinder academic terminology, to transition to a more mature state as strategically best fitted its evolving operating environment. It would be in nobody's interest for Tesla to regress to a bygone era of organizational structure and style, but the very real possibility of executive succession alone painted a picture of likely chaos. Nevertheless, something had to happen, and the project management literature is rich with ideas for all modern industries, companies, and situations.

Corporate cash flow is largely determined by capital project FCFs. There, project cost risks derive from project hurdle rates, which derive from the cost of capital itself. To close the circle, cost of capital is a function of other kinds of project risk. This all "happens" at the nexus of capital planning and project management. These are the foremost points in this series.

Questions for Discussion

How does the *evolution* of external conditions impact organizational form and function?

How can risks (see section subtitles) impact capital project hurdle rates?

Is a diversified project portfolio the best approach to technological uncertainty?

Media Articles

Alton, L. 2018. "Why Batteries are Holding Up Tech Breakthroughs — And What's Happening Now." *Next Web*, February 21.

Assis, C. 2016. "Moment of Truth Arrives for Tesla, Elon Musk." *MarketWatch*, March 3.

Assis, C. 2019. "Tesla's 2019 Challenge? To Remain Profitable Quarter After Quarter." *MarketWatch*, January 2.

Baer, D. 2014. "The Making of Tesla: Invention, Betrayal, and the Birth of the Roadster." *Business Insider*, November 11.

Barrabi, T. 2018. "Tesla Shareholders to Vote on Ousting Elon Musk as Chairman." *FOXBusiness*, May 1.

Barrabi, T. 2018. "Tesla CEO Elon Musk Takes Over Model 3 Production as Stock Slides." *FOXBusiness*, April 02.

Bartz, D. 2014. "FTC Officials Back Tesla's Direct-To-Consumer Car Sales Model." *Reuters*, April 24.

Berman, B. 2016. "Here's Why You Might be an Electric Car Owner a Decade from Now". *Technology Review*, March 30.

Bomey, N. 2016. "Tesla's Stock Rises as Model 3 Preorders Near 200,000." *USA TODAY*, April 01.

Bomey, N. 2017. "Why Mazda is Betting on a Gas Engine Breakthrough." *USA Today*, August 1.

Bomey, N. 2017. "Tesla to Begin Selling Solar Roof Tiles." *USA Today*, May 10.

Boston, W. 2016. "Carmakers Rev Up Push into Electric Vehicles." Wall Street Journal, September 29.

Carey, N. 2017. "Consumer Reports Says Tesla Misunderstands 'Positive' Model 3 Rating." *Reuters*, October 20.

DeBord, M. 2017. "There's a Potentially Devastating New Twist in the Tesla Story." *Business Insider*, August 13.

Durbin, D. 2017. "GM Raises Output of Self-Driving Bolts, Boosts Test Fleet." *AP*, June 13.

Eisenstein, P.A. 2018. "From Cellphones to Cars, These Batteries Could Cut the Cord Forever." *NBC*, January 1.

Eisenstein, P.A. "Tesla Recalls Almost Half the Cars It Ever Built, As Shares Tank and Musk's Billions Shrink." *NBC*, March 30, 2018.

Eisenstein, P.A. 2011a. "Carmakers Enjoy Electric Buzz — Within Reason." *msnbc.com*, January 12. 2011-01-12T13:37:35

Eisenstein, P.A. 2011b. "Nissan Leaf Electric Car." *msnbc.com*, nd.

Franck, T. 2018. "Goldman: Tesla Must Raise $10 Billion in 2 Years to Survive." *CNBC*, May 17.

Heisler, Y. 2018. "Elon Musk Wants Model 3 Production to Hit 7,000 Units Per Week Before December." *BGR*, November 16.

Higgins, T., and S. Pulliam. 2018. "Elon Musk Races to Exit Tesla's Production Hell." *Wall Street Journal*, June 28.

Higgins, T., and S. Pulliam. 2018. "Tesla's Make-Or-Break Moment is Fast Approaching." *Wall Street Journal*, March 15.

Hoium, T. 2016. "The 5 Best-Selling Electric Cars of 2016." *Motley Fool*, December 03.

Hull, D. 2018. "Tesla Urges Workers to Disprove Critics, Ramp Up Production." *Bloomberg*, March 29.

Hull, D. 2018. "Tesla Breaks Another Production Promise with Crucial Model 3." *Bloomberg*, January 3.

Kageyama, Y. 2017. "Toyota Planning 10 Purely Electric Vehicles by 2020s." *AP*, December 18.

Kharpal, A. 2017. "Musk: Tesla will Begin Taking Orders for Glass Solar Roof Tiles from Today." *CNBC*, May 10.

Krishner, T. 2018. "Tesla Makes 5,000 Model 3s Per Week, But Can It Continue?" *AP*, July 2.

Matousek, M. 2018. "Tesla Has Left Salespeople Confused Over When Customers will Get the Powerwall and Solar Roof." *Business Insider*, June 26.

McGee, P. 2017. "Volkswagen Plans to 'Leapfrog' Tesla in Electric Car Race." *Financial Times*, May 7.

McGee, P. 2019. "Volkswagen Turns to Tesla for Recharging Stations." *Financial Times*, February 4.

McKenna, F. 2018. "Tesla Says It Did Not Ask Suppliers for Cash Back." *MarketWatch*, July 24.

McLaughlin, K. 2015. "Tesla Raises Offering to About 2.7 Million Shares." *Bloomberg*, August 14.

Mims, C. 2018. "The Battery Boost We've Waited for is Only a Few Years Out." *Wall Street Journal*, March 18.

Mui, Y. 2017. "States Yank Electric-Car Incentives, Add Infrastructure Fees." *CNBC*, July 03.

Mukherjee, S. 2018. "Tesla Shares, Bonds Drop as CEO Musk Bites Hand of Wall Street." *Reuters*, May 3.

Muoio, D. 2017. "Mercedes is Quietly Becoming Tesla's Biggest Rival." *Business Insider*, November 12.

Muoio, D. 2017. "Tesla Completely Missed Its Goal for Model 3 Production in Sept." *Business Insider*, October 02.

Naughton, K. 2012. "Hybrids' Unlikely Rival: Plain Old Cars." *Bloomberg*, February 23.

No author. 2017. "BMW: 12 New Electric Cars to Challenge Tesla. "*Motley Fool*, September 7.

No author. 2018. "China Auto Show Highlights Industry's Electric Ambitions." *AP*, April 22.

No author. 2018. "France's PSA Group to Offer 40 Electric Vehicles by 2025." *AP*, January 17.

No author. 2018. "Lithium ETF Powers Down on Morgan Stanley's Dismal Forecast." *ETF Trends*, February 26.

No author. 2016. "Tesla Inks Deal to Buy German Manufacturing Engineering Firm." *AP*, November 08.

No author. 2018. "Tesla's Second-Quarter Deliveries in 2 Wild Charts." *Motley Fool*, July 2.

No author. 2017. "Where the World's Biggest Automakers are Investing for the Future." *FOXBusiness*, October 12.

No author. 2017. "BMW's Sleek Electric Sedan will Challenge Tesla." *Motley Fool*, September 13.

No author. 2017. "Chevrolet Bolt Deliveries Hit New High." *Motley Fool*, July 3.

No author. 2017. "Honda is Finally Getting Serious About Electric Cars." *Motley Fool*, September 14.

No author. 2018. "How Tesla's Elon Musk Could Become the World's Richest Man Without Ever Getting a Paycheck." *Fortune*, January 22.

No author. 2018. "Musk Suggests Tesla's New Chairwoman Won't Rein Him In." *AP*, December 10.

No author. 2019. "Read the Email Musk Sent to Tesla Employees Explaining Job Cuts." *CNBC*, January 18.

No author. 2019. "Tesla Has Over 3,000 Model 3s Left in US Inventory: Electrek."

No author. 2017. "Tesla in 'Production Hell' To Meet Model 3 Deadline: Elon Musk." *Reuters*, October 7.

No author. 2019. "Tesla Produced 61,394 Model 3s in Fourth Quarter." *Reuters*, January 2.

No author. 2017. "Tesla Said to Reach Pact with Shanghai for China Production." *Bloomberg*, June 22.

No author. 2017. "Tesla Says Its Model 3 Car will go on Sale on Friday." *AP*, July 3.

No author. 2019. "Tesla to Cut Workforce by 7%." *Reuters*, January 18.

No author. 2008. "Tesla to Start Production in China Next Year, Shanghai Says." *Bloomberg*, December 5.

No author. 2012. "Tesla Unveils Faster Electric Car Charging Station." *AP*, September 25.

No author. 2017. "VW is 'Second Mover' in Electric Commercial Vehicles: Executive." *Reuters*, September 17.

No author. 2017. "BMW's Sleek Electric Sedan will Challenge Tesla." *Motley Fool*, September 13.

No author. 2017. "Chevrolet Bolt Deliveries Hit New High." *Motley Fool*, July 3.

No author. 2017. "China Looks at Ending Sales of Gasoline Cars." *AP*, September 10.

No author. 2017. "Honda is Finally Getting Serious About Electric Cars." *Motley Fool*, September 14.

No author. 2017. "New Technology Could Make Solar Panels Cheaper, More Accessible." *The Daily Dot*, May 19.

No author. 2017. "Tesla Deliveries at Low End of Forecast, Starting Model 3 Production." *Reuters*, July 2.

No author. 2017. "Tesla Says Its Model 3 Car will Go on Sale on Friday." *AP*, July 3.

No author. 2018. "Tesla Sticks by Model 3 Target, Posts Worst Ever Quarterly Loss," *Reuters*, February 6.

No author. 2017. "Tesla Truck Unveiled (Wow!): 8 Key Things You Should Know." *Motley Fool*, November 17.

No author. 2017. "Tesla's Elon Musk Offers to Solve Power Crisis in South Australia." *Reuters*, March 10.

No author. 2018. "Tesla's Second-Quarter Deliveries in 2 Wild Charts." *Motley Fool*, July 2.

No author. 2018. "Volkswagen to Devote 3 German Plants to Electric Car Push." *AP*, November 14.

Olinga, L. 2016. "Tesla Bulks Up on IT Talent for 'Car of the Future' Fight." *AFP*, January 13.

Paul, S. 2017. "Tesla's Big Battery Races to Keep South Australia's Lights on." *Reuters*, September 28.

Pikkarainen, J. 2016. "What Tesla's New Gigafactory Means for Electric Vehicles." *TechCrunch*, November 06.

Poletti, T. 2016. "Elon Musk's Pedestal is Crumbling, Exposing Tesla Risks." *MarketWatch*, July 12.

Randall, T. 2018. "'The Last Bet-the-Company Situation': Q&A with Elon Musk." *Bloomberg*, July 13.

Rocco, M. 2015. "Tesla Readies Model X for Long-Awaited Debut." *FOXBusiness*, September 29.

Rocco, M. 2018a. "Electric Truck Maker Nikola to Build $1B Plant in Arizona." *Fox Business*, January 30.

Rocco, M. 2018b. "Tesla Rival Nikola Wins Anheuser-Busch Electric Truck Order." *Fox Business*, May 03.

Rodriguez, S. 2018. "Electric Vehicles Seen Driving Cobalt Crunch by Mid-2020s." *Business News*, May 24.

Rosevar, J. 2018. "This Electric Semi is Trucking Right Past Tesla's." *Motley Fool*, June 28.

Rosevear, J. 2017. "General Motors is Betting $600 Million on Self-Driving this Year." *Markets Fool*, April 08.

Sage, A. 2018. "Tesla Plans Six-Day Stoppage at Factory for Assembly Line Fixes: Sources." *Reuters*, May 15.

Sage, A., and S. Rodriguez. 2018. "Exclusive: Tesla Hits Model 3 Manufacturing Milestone, Hours After Deadline - Factory Sources." *Reuters*, July 1.

Sage, A. 2018. "Tesla Plans Six-Day Stoppage at Factory for Assembly Line Fixes: Sources." *Reuters*, May 15.

Sage, A. 2017a. "Tesla Unveils Electric Big-Rig Truck, Sporty Roadster." *Reuters*, November 17.

Sage, A., and E. Taylor. 2018. "Exclusive: Tesla Flies in New Battery Production Line for Gigafactory." *Reuters*, May 25.

Sage, A., and S. Rodriguez. 2018. "Exclusive: Tesla Hits Model 3 Manufacturing Milestone, Hours After Deadline - Factory Sources." *Reuters*, July 1.

Sage, A., and S. Rodriguez. 2018. "Shouting CEO, Changing Rules: Inside Tesla's Model 3-Building Sprint." *Reuters*, July 2.

Shane, D. 2017. "China is Winning Electric Cars 'Arms Race'." *CNN*, November 20.

Sharma, B. 2018. "SEC Subpoenas Tesla on Model 3 Production Estimates." *Reuters*, November 2.

Shepardson, D. 1919. "GM Said to Hit 200,000 U.S. Electric Vehicles Sold in 2018." *Reuters*, January 2.

Shepardson, D. 2019. "Tesla Urges Tariff Exemption for Chinese-Made Car Computer." *Reuters*, January 4.

Shepardson, D. 2019. "Report: GM's Cadillac Will Introduce EV In Fight Against Tesla." *Reuters*. January 10.

Siegel, M. 2015. "Tesla Says Australian Utility Origin to Market Solar Battery." *Reuters*, December 30.

Sparks, D. 2016. "Tesla Motors, Inc. Shines in Consumer Reports Survey." *Motley Fool*, December 30.

Sparks, D. 2017. "Tesla Motors, Inc.'s Vehicle Deliveries Miss Guidance -- What Investors Should Know." *Markets Fool*, January 03.

Sparks, D. 2017b. "Tesla Stock Nears $300: What Investors Need to Know. " *Markets Fool*, April 03.

Sparks, D. 2017a. "Tesla's Gigafactory Doubles in Size, Brings Battery Cell Production to U.S." *Markets Fool*, January 04.

Stafford, J. 2016. "Tesla, Tech Icons Scramble for Lithium as Prices Double." *USA TODAY*, April 14.

Summers, N. 2018. "Will Tesla Open Up Its Supercharger Network in Europe?" *Endagadget*, November 16.

Taylor, E. 2019. "Volkswagen to Cut Up To 7,000 Jobs in New Savings Drive." *Reuters*. March 13.

Tepper, T. 2017. "How Tesla Became the Most Valuable Car Company in the U.S." *Money*, June 8.

Tobak, S. 2016. "Why Tesla Model 3 will be Elon Musk's Undoing." *FOXBusiness*, August 04.

Vance, A. 2012. "Tesla's Magic Elon Musk, The 21st Century Industrialist." *BusinessWeek*, September 13.

Vartabedian, M. 2017. "Tesla's Electric Big Rig Aims for 200 To 300 Miles on a Charge." *Reuters*, August 24.

Williams, P. 2017. "Elon Musk's Giant Battery Set for Testing in South Australia." *Bloomberg*, November 22.

Woodyard, C. 2015. "Tesla Prices Novel Model X SUV at $80,000." *USA Today*, November 23.

References

Abernathy, W.J., and J.M. Utterback. 1988. "Patterns of Industrial Innovation." *Strategic Management of Technology and Innovation*, eds. R.A. Burgelman and M.A. Maidique. Homewood: Irwin.

Adjaoud, F., D. Charfi, and L. Chourou. 2011. "Corporate Governance and Investment Decisions." In *Capital Budgeting Valuation: Financial Analysis for Today's Investment Projects*, eds. H.K. Baker and P. English. USA: Wiley.

Andrews, K.R. 1987. *The Concept of Corporate Strategy*. Homewood: Irwin.

Armstrong, G., and P. Kotler. 2002. *Marketing: An Introduction*, 6th ed. Upper Saddle River NJ: Prentice-Hall.

Arnold, T., and T. Nixon. 2011. "Measuring Investment Value: Free Cash Flow, Net Present Value, and Economic Value-Added." In *Capital Budgeting Valuation: Financial Analysis for Today's Investment Projects*, eds. H.K. Baker and P. English. USA: Wiley.

Baker, H.K., and P. English. 2011. "Capital Budgeting: An Overview." In *Capital Budgeting Valuation: Financial Analysis for Today's Investment Projects*, eds. H.K. Baker and P. English. USA: Wiley.

Barnard, C. 1938. *The Functions of the Executive*. Cambridge: Harvard University Press.

Besanko, D., D. Dranove, and M. Shanley. 2000. *Economics of Strategy*, 2nd ed. New York, NY: John Wiley.

Bierman, H., and S. Schmidt. 2006. *The Capital Budgeting Decision*. New York, NY: Routledge.

Biondi, Y., and G. Marzo. 2011. "Decision Making Using Behavioral Finance for Capital Budgeting." In *Capital Budgeting Valuation: Financial Analysis for Today's Investment Projects*, eds. H.K. Baker and P. English. USA: Wiley.

Block, Z., and I. MacMillan. 1995. *Corporate Venturing: Creating New Businesses Within the Firm*. Boston: Harvard Business School Press.

Blois, K.J. 1996. "Vertical Quasi-Integration." In *Firms, Organizations and Contracts*, eds. P.J. Buckley and J. Michie. New York, NY: Oxford University Press.

Brentani, U., and E.J. Kleinschmidt. Febraury/March 2015. "The Impact of Company Resources and Capabilities on Global New Product Program Performance." *Project Management Journal* 46, no. 1, pp. 12–29.

Buckley, P.J., and M. Casson. 1996. "Joint Ventures." In *Firms, Organizations and Contracts*, eds. P.J. Buckley and J. Michie. New York, NY: Oxford University Press.

Burgelman, R.A., and L.R. Sayles. 1986. *Inside Corporate Innovation*. New York, NY: Free Press.

Cleland, D.I., and L.R. Ireland. 2002. *Project Management: Strategic Design and Implementation*. New York, NY: McGraw-Hill.

Cohen, D.J., and R.J. Graham. 2001. *The Project Manager's MBA: How to Translate Project Decisions into Business Success*. San Francisco: Wiley.

Collyer, S. December/January 2017. "Culture, Communication, and Leadership for Projects in Dynamic Environments." *Project Management Journal* 47, no. 6, pp. 111–125.

Daft, R.L. 2004. *Organization Theory and Design*, 8th ed. USA: Thomson South-Western.

Eskerod, P., M. Huemann, and G. Ringhofer. January 2016. "Project Stakeholder Management – Past and Present." *Project Management Journal* 46, no. 6, pp. 42–54.

Eskerod, P., M. Huemann, and G. Savage. January 2016. "Project Stakeholder Management—Past and Present." *Project Management Journal* 46, no. 6, pp. 6–14.

Fairtlough, G. 1994. "Innovation and Organization." In *The Handbook of Industrial Innovation*, eds. M. Dodgson and R. Rothwell. Cornwall, England: Edward Edgar Publishing Company.

Fernholz, F.R. 2011. "Multicriteria Analysis for Capital Budgeting." In *Capital Budgeting Valuation: Financial Analysis for Today's Investment Projects*, eds. H.K. Baker and P. English. USA: Wiley.

Ferreira, D. 2011. "Corporate Strategy and Investment Decisions." In *Capital Budgeting Valuation: Financial Analysis for Today's Investment Projects*, eds. H.K. Baker and P. English. USA: Wiley.

Grant, R.M. 2002. *Contemporary Strategy Analysis: Concepts, Techniques, Applications*, 4th ed. USA: Blackwell.

Greasley, A. 2006. *Operations Management*. New York, NY: John Wiley.

Hamel, G., and C.K. Prahalad. 1994. *Competing for the Future*. Boston: Harvard Business School Press.

Hart, O. 1993. "An Economist's Perspective on the Theory of the Firm." In *Firms, Organizations and Contracts*, eds. P.J. Buckley and J. Michie. New York, NY: Oxford University Press.

Heerkens, G. 2006. *The Business-Savvy Project Manager: Indispensable Knowledge and Skills for Success*. New York, NY: McGraw-Hill.

Heizer, J., and B. Render. 2005. *Operations Management*, 7th ed. Upper Saddle River NJ: Pearson Prentice-Hall.

Kerzner, H. 2009. *Project Management Best Practices: Achieving Global Excellence*. New York, NY: John Wiley.

Killen, C.P., R.A. Hunt, and E.J. Kleinschmidt. 2008. "Learning Investments and Organizational Capabilities: Case Studies in the Development of Project Portfolio Management Capabilities." *International Journal of Managing Projects in Business* 1, no. 3, pp. 334–51.

Mariti, P., and R.H. Smiley. 1996. "Co-operative Agreements and the Organization of Industry." In *Firms, Organizations and Contracts*, eds. P.J. Buckley, and J. Michie. New York, NY: Oxford University Press.

Martinsuo, M., and C.P. Killen. October/November 2014. "Value Management in Project Portfolios: Identifying and Addressing Strategic Value." *Project Management Journal* 45, no. 5, pp. 56–70.

McGrath, R.N. 1996. *Technological Discontinuities and Institutional Legitimacy: A Morphological Perspective*. UMI Dissertation Services.

McGrath, R.N. 2012. *Project-Driven Technology Strategy*. Newtown Sq. PA: Project Management institute.

Mohr, J., S. Sengupta, and S. Slater. 2005. *Marketing of High-Technology Products and Innovations,* 2d ed. Upper Saddle River NJ: Pearson Prentice-Hall.

Mukherjee, N., and N.M. Al Rahahleh. 2011. "Capital Budgeting Techniques in Practise: U.S. Survey Evidence." In *Capital Budgeting Valuation: Financial Analysis for Today's Investment Projects,* eds. H.K. Baker and P. English. USA: Wiley.

Muller, R., J.R. Turner, E.S. Andersen, J. Shao, and O. Kvalnes. December/ January 2017. "Governance and Ethics in Temporary Organizations: The Mediating Role of Corporate Governance." *Project Management Journal* 47, no. 6, pp. 7–24.

PMI-Competency. 2017. *Project Management Competency Development Framework,* 3rd ed. Newtown Square PA: Project Management Institute.

PMI-PMBOK. 2017. *A Guide to the Project Management Body of Knowledge: PMBOK Guide,* 6th ed. Newtown Square PA: Project Management Institute.

Porter, M.E. 1980. *Competitive Strategy: Techniques for Analyzing Industries and Competitors.* New York, NY: Free Press.

Prahalad, C.K., and G. Hamel. 1994. "Strategy as a Field of Study: Why search for a New Paradigm?" *Strategic Management Journal* 15, pp. 5–16.

Quinn, J.B. 1980. *Strategies for Change: Logical Incrementalism.* Homewood: Irwin.

Rothwell, R., and M. Dodgson. 1994. "Innovation and Size of Firm." In *The Handbook of Industrial Innovation*, eds. M. Dodgson and R. Rothwell. Cornwall, England: Edward Elgar Publishing Company.

Sako, M. 1994. "Supplier Relationships and Innovation." In *The Handbook of Industrial Innovation,* eds. M. Dodgson and R. Rothwell. Cornwall, England: Edward Elgar Publishing Company.

Schiffer, M.B. 1994. *Taking Charge: The Electric Automobile in America*. USA: Smithsonian.

Schilling, M.A. 2005. *Strategic Management of Technological Innovation*. New York, NY: McGraw-Hill Irwin.

Schumpeter, J.A. 1976. *Capitalism, Socialism, and Democracy*. New York, NY: Harper and Row.

Scott, W.R. 1993. *Organizations: Rational, Natural, and Open Systems*. Englewood Cliffs, NJ: Prentice-Hall.

Sharifi, M.M., and M. Safari. August/September 2016. "Application of Net Cash Flow at Risk in Project Portfolio Selection." *Project Management Journal* 47, no.4, pp. 68–78.

Shnayerson, M. 1996. *The Car that Could: The Inside Story of GM's Revolutionary Electric Vehicle*. USA: Random House.

Sicotte, H., N. Drouin, and H. Delerue. January 2014. "Innovation Portfolio Management as a Subset of Dynamic Capabilities: Measurement and Impact on Innovation Performance." *Project Management Journal* 45, no. 6, pp. 58–72.

Stevenson, W.J. 2009. *Operations Management*, 10th ed. New York, NY: McGraw-Hill Irwin.

Teller, J., A. Kock, and H.G. Gemunden. 2014. "Risk Management in Project Portfolios is More Than Managing Project Risks: A Contingency Perspective on Risk Management." *Project Management Journal* 45, no. 4, pp. 67–80.

Tidd, J., J. Bessant, and K. Pavitt. 2001. *Managing Innovation: Integrating Technological, Market and Organizational Change*, 2nd ed. New York, NY: Wiley.

Tirole, J. 1990. *The Theory of Industrial Organization*. Cambridge: MIT Press.

Tushman, M.L., and P.A. Anderson. 1986. "Technological Discontinuities and Organizational Environments." *Administrative Science Quarterly* 31, pp. 439–65.

Tyran, M.R. 1991. *The Vest-Pocket Guide to Business Ratios*. Englewood-Cliffs: Prentice-Hall.

Wakefield, E.H. 1994. *History of the Electric Automobile*. USA: Society of Automotive Engineers.

Wren, D.W. 2003. *The History of Management Thought*, 5th ed. USA: Wiley & Sons.

About the Author

Dr. Robert N. McGrath, PhD, MBA, PMP. Bob began his career by graduating from the U.S. Air Force Academy and served five years as an Aircraft Maintenance and Explosive Ordnance Disposal Officer. Afterward, he worked in project-driven aerospace environments as a logistician, engineer, and manager for Texas Instruments, General Electric Aircraft Engines, and the Lockheed Aeronautical Systems Company. When the Cold War ended and with several Master's Degrees accomplished, he completed a PhD in Business Administration at the Louisiana State University.

As a full-time business administration and project management academic, he has served as an MBA or EMBA Program Director and the Director of the largest online project management curriculum in the world. His scholarship and teaching have focused mainly in the areas of strategic management, project management, technology and innovation management, operations management, and logistics. He has published over 75 scholarly, pedagogical, and practitioner items in an attempt to bridge the gap between the fields that must function together in highly competitive organizations. In 2007, he became certificated as a PMI Project Management Professional (PMP), teaching mostly online in that field for the remainder of his career. He is now retired to continue writing in his areas of interest.

This three-volume series is a culmination of work that started in1993. His 1996 PhD dissertation addressed the electric vehicle industry of that day, constructing a content analysis of 2,000 media items for biases for and against various battery technologies, as theory would predict. The events that have transpired since 1996 are consistent with the findings and conclusions in that dissertation, motivating further study, that have culminated in this book.

Index

Alphabets '*e*' and '*t*' in italics after page number indicate 'exhibit' and 'table', respectively.

AC Propulsion, 1
angel investor, 67

battery, 22
  lithium ion, 17, 20
  technology development in, 17–19
brand capital, 5
business strategy, 28
  and competitive advantage, 28–29
  and economic profit, 29
  and profitability, 28

capability portfolio, 22, 25
capital projects, 34, 36, 39, 43, 72,
    97, 105, 109
  and costs, 107
  goal of, 97
  and hurdle rate, 72
  management of, 40
  and organizational breakdown
    structure (OBS), 105
  and project charter, 100–101
  project lifecycle, 113
  schedule delays in, 106
  strategic concern of, 98
capital risk
  liquidity risk, 32
  principal risk, 32
  return risk, 32
corporate governance, 65, 66. *See*
    also decision-making,
    executive
  angel investor, 67
  and communication, importance
    of, 65
  decision-making flaws, reasons for,
    70–71
  economic interpretation of, 69

  and effect of initial public offering
    (IPO) on private capital,
    67–69
  and free cash flow, 77
  and herding behaviour, 75
  hurdle rate and decision-making,
    72
  information asymmetry and
    decision-making, 69–70,
    73, 76
  and insider ownership, 73–74, 78
  and managerial compensation
    issues, 78–79
  pre-IPO vs. pot-IPO
    expectations, 68
  private capital, 67
  and role of board of directors
    (BOD), 69, 70, 73, 74,
    75, 76
  role of managers in, 71, 72, 73
corporate management. *See also*
    corporate strategy; project
    communication
  measures of success
    capital cost and risks, 31–32
    discount vs. hurdle rate, 33
    free cash flow, 33–34
    opportunity cost of capital,
      32–33
    return on investment (ROI), 31
  vs. project management, 30–31
corporate portfolio, 16, 25, 28, 30,
    31, 34, 69
  and financial portfolio, 16, 30
  vs. project portfolio, 34
corporate strategy, 25, 90, 106.
    See also decision-making,
    executive
  vs. business strategy, 28

and capabilities, 25
and communication management, 65
and public equity, 68
and shareholder wealth, 29–30, 73
and technology innovation, 52
corporation, 25, 28, 30, 32, 92
characteristics of, 25

decision-making, executive
anchoring effects in, 83
cash flow bias, 86
commitment to failure, effect on, 88–89
expense vs. investment on, 87–88
framing effects in, 83, 84, 85
inductive fallacy in, 82
judgement default, 81
managerial bias in, 81
role of inflation in, 84–85
discount rate, 33, 84, 85, 86, 92, 107
discounted cash flow (DCF), 36

earned value management (EVM), 107–108
purpose of, 107
Eberhard, Martin, 1, 3
economic profit. See economic value added (EVA)
economic value added (EVA), 29, 32, 37, 51, 97, 98, 107, 110, 119, 135
electric vehicle (EV), 1, 3, 4, 5, 7, 10, 12, 17, 20, 53, 82, 121, 122, 127

Ford, 1, 7
free cash flow (FCF), 33–34, 36, 47, 49, 73, 77, 79, 86, 97, 102, 107, 135
and discounted cash flow (DCF), 36
vs. operating cash flow, 34–35

General Motors, 1, 7, 8

hurdle rate, 33, 72, 92, 107

inductive fallacy, 82
industry lifecycle (ILC), 52, 55
as a management framework, 53
phases in, 53, 54t
and principal-agent theory, 70, 80, 88
and product lifecycle (PLC), 53
and technology innovation, 52, 52t
internal corporate venturing (ICV)
and external collaboration, 59–61, 60t
goal of, 56, 57
meaning, 56
objectives, 57
organizational structure, 58t
risks in, 58

mainstream segments, 29
Model 3, 7, 8, 10, 13
Model D, 7
Model S, 5, 6, 7
Model X, 5
multicriteria assessment (MCA)
criteria for, 49, 50–51
importance of, 48
planning process in, 50
scoring factors and targets in, 51t
Musk, Elon, 1, 2, 3, 4, 7, 11, 12, 24, 28, 50, 54, 67, 73, 75, 80, 121

operating projects, 34

pioneer markets, 29
price point, 14
principal-agent theory, 70
private capital, 67
product life cycle (PLC), 53
project communication
and documentation, 66
formal communication issues in, 66
importance of, 64
issues with, 65
role of bureaucracy, 66
project management
as an organizing principle, 92
constrained nature of projects, 97–98

definition of a project, 96
earned value management (EVM),
    107–108
and functional organization, 93–94
and matrix organization, 95–96
plan, 102, 103
PMI and capital project finance, 91
and project charter, 100–101, 103
and project cost, 107
project deadlines, 97,98
and project integration, 99
and Project Management Institute
    (PMI), 91
project quality management,
    108–110
project scope statement and project
    lifecycle, 103, 113
project scope, 102–103
project uniqueness, 97, 109
and pure project organization, 94–95
resources management, 110–111
and risk management, 100,
    113–118
and schedules, 105–106
statement of work (SOW), 101
supply chain in, 118–119
work breakdown structure (WBS)
    and project deliverables,
    103–105
Project Management Body of
    Knowledge (PMBOK), 39,
    66, 91, 101, 102, 108, 113
and Project Management Office
    (PMO), 39
Project Management Institute (PMI),
    43, 47, 91, 110
and project definition, 96
and Project Management
    Professional (PMP), 91
Project Management Office (PMO)
as a management structure, 40
definition, 39
project portfolio management
    (PPM), 40, 41
purpose of, 41
roles and responsibilities of, 41e
project portfolio management (PPM),
    40

project portfolio, 31, 39
multicriteria assessment in, 48–51
and project portfolio management
    (PPM) capability, 40–41
proposal appraisal
evaluation, 47
implementation, 47
post-completion audit, 48
project estimate and cash flow,
    47
proposal screening, 47
selection, 47
proposal development, 43, 44e
and technology innovation, 52
project risk management
objective, 114
probability matrix in, 117t
risk definition, 113
risk dimensions in, 116
project stakeholder, 29, 30, 63, 65,
    66, 73. See also project
    communication

return on investment (ROI), 31
cash inflow vs. cash outflow, 31,
    32, 34
Roadster, 2, 3, 4, 26, 49

Smith, Malcom, 1
SpaceX, 2
strategic management, 15.
    See also corporate
    strategy; project
    communication
economies of sale, 21
and exemplary corporation, 25
hedging as a strategy, 21
importance in business, 15
of supply chain, 25
of technologies, 24
product market vs. organization
    competencies and
    capabilities, 22
and technology development,
    16–17, 18, 19, 21
and technology innovation, 52
timing of technology development,
    22

Tarpenning, Marc, 1
technology innovation, 52
Tesla Motor Inc., *See* Tesla
Tesla, 1, 2, 8, 10, 12, 13, 20, 24, 28,
        40, 53, 63, 80, 85, 121
    battery issues, 6, 122
    capital issues, 10–11, 12, 124
    contracting risks, 130, 132
    cost issues, 122
    electric vehicles, issues with, 1–2,
        122
    hybrid cars, 8
    inception days, 1–2
    initial public offering, 4
    Model 3, 7, 8, 10, 13
Model D, 7
Model S, 5, 6, 7
Model X, 5
procurement risks, 125–128
production issues, 3, 4, 5, 10
range issues, 6, 122
and Roadster, 2, 3, 4, 26, 49
supply chain, 5–6, 125
technology risks, 19, 130
Tesla Semi, 25–26

U.S. Securities and Exchange
        Commission (EC), 12

Wright, Ian, 2

OTHER TITLES IN THE PORTFOLIO AND PROJECT MANAGEMENT COLLECTION

Timothy J. Kloppenborg, Xavier University, Editor

- *Agile Working and the Digital Workspace* by John Eary
- *Passion, Persistence, and Patience* by Alfonso Bucero
- *Adaptive Project Planning* by Louise Worsley and Christopher Worsley
- *The Lost Art of Planning Projects* by Louise Worsley and Christopher Worsley
- *Project Communication from Start to Finish* by Geraldine E. Hynes

Announcing the Business Expert Press Digital Library

Concise e-books business students need for classroom and research

This book can also be purchased in an e-book collection by your library as

- a one-time purchase,
- that is owned forever,
- allows for simultaneous readers,
- has no restrictions on printing, and
- can be downloaded as PDFs from within the library community.

Our digital library collections are a great solution to beat the rising cost of textbooks. E-books can be loaded into their course management systems or onto students' e-book readers.
The **Business Expert Press** digital libraries are very affordable, with no obligation to buy in future years. For more information, please visit **www.businessexpertpress.com/librarians**. To set up a trial in the United States, please email **sales@businessexpertpress.com**.